Consider the Lilies Scottish Painting 1910–1980
from the Collection of the City of Dundee

A National Galleries of Scotland Partnership Project
with McManus Galleries and Museum, Dundee

Alice Strang

CONSIDER THE LILIES

Scottish Painting 1910–1980
from the Collection of the City of Dundee

McManus Galleries and Museum
Dundee City Council
in association with
National Galleries of Scotland
Edinburgh · 2006

Published by Dundee City Council, Leisure and
Communities Department, on the occasion of the exhibition
*Consider the Lilies: Scottish Painting 1910–1980 from the
Collection of the City of Dundee*, held at the Dean Gallery,
Edinburgh from 28 October 2006 to 14 January 2007 and
at The Fleming Collection, London from 25 January to
5 April 2007, to mark the redevelopment and reopening of
McManus Galleries and Museum, Dundee in 2008.

ISBN 0 900344 61 X / 978 0 900344 61 9

Designed by Dalrymple
Typeset in Stone Humanist and Penumbra
Printed in Dundee by D. C. Thomson & Co. Ltd

Front cover: James McIntosh Patrick *The Tay Bridge from
my Studio Window*, 1948 [detail]
Frontispiece: John Quinton Pringle *Portrait of May
(Mary Boyd)*, 1923 [detail]
Back cover: Artist's impression of the environmental
improvements to Albert Square, Dundee

FOREWORD

Consider the Lilies is a double celebration; of Dundee's collection of Scottish art from the period 1910 to 1980, and of the restoration of McManus Galleries and Museum, through the most ambitious renovation project in the building's history. The title of the exhibition derives from a painting by Peter Collins (see p.37), and also acknowledges Dundee's coat of arms, the pot of three lilies symbolising the Virgin Mary, the City's patron saint.

McManus Galleries and Museum is housed in a Victorian Gothic revival building dating back to 1867. It closed to the public in October 2005 and reopens with facilities befitting a twenty-first century visitor attraction in 2008. This closure provided the opportunity to show a selection of Dundee's finest modern Scottish paintings at the Dean Gallery, Edinburgh and at The Fleming Collection, London and led to the creation of this permanent collection publication.

The project has been a partnership between the National Galleries of Scotland and McManus Galleries and Museum and we are particularly grateful to the director of the Scottish National Gallery of Modern Art, Richard Calvocoressi, and to Janis Adams, Norrie Colston, James Holloway, Steve Johnstone, Susan Keracher, Vicki Marshall, Elaine Milne, Eileen Murison, Lauren Rigby, Anna Robertson, Jo Sage, Alice Strang, Christine Thompson and Clara Young for their hard work and enthusiasm, which has resulted in its successful achievement.

Our thanks are also due to all the staff of both institutions, who have been involved with *Consider the Lilies*, as well as to the many external people who have assisted in various ways with the exhibition and publication. We are especially indebted to the living artists featured, who have all provided statements about their works, namely John Bellany, Dennis Buchan, Peter Collins, John Houston, James Howie, Jack Knox, Will Maclean and James Morrison. Relatives and acquaintances of artists no longer alive have also provided vital information. Senga Davidson generously shared her research into the Tayport Artists' Circle and Stewart Carmichael in particular, whilst the following went beyond the call of duty in helping with research: Chloë Blackburn, Margaret Carlaw, Nicola Ireland, Matthew Jarron, Dr Margaret McCance, Robin McClure, James B. Mackellar, John McLean, Professor David Michie, Lady Philipson, Dr Alastair Robertson Ross, Joanna Soden and Bill Taylor. Selina Skipwith and her colleagues at Flemings have participated in the project with customary zeal and we are delighted that through their efforts Dundee's masterpieces will be shown to a London audience.

Works could not join the collection without the help of the many benefactors of McManus Galleries and Museum. They range from individuals who have made gifts and bequests, to bodies such as the National Fund for Acquisitions, The Art Fund, Contemporary Art Society and the Scottish Arts Council. The long-term financial assistance provided by sources such as the Morris Trust Fund and Ower Bequest Fund has resulted in the acquisition of many important works.

The re-development of McManus Galleries and Museum would not be possible without generous funding from the Heritage Lottery Fund, Historic Scotland, the European Regional Development Fund and Dundee City Council. We are extremely grateful to them all.

We hope that the *Consider the Lilies* exhibition and publication will attract new friends and supporters to Dundee to visit the diverse collections and refurbished McManus Galleries and Museum. We also look forward to future partnerships between McManus and the National Galleries of Scotland, bringing the wealth of Scottish art to the people of Scotland and our visitors from around the world.

JOHN STEWART-YOUNG
Project Director, McManus Galleries and Museum

JOHN LEIGHTON
Director-General, National Galleries of Scotland

George Leslie Hunter, *Still Life*, c.1918 [detail]

FUNDERS

The *Who We Are* project will restore McManus Galleries and Museum, redisplay its collections and provide a new entrance and visitor facilities to create a twenty-first century museum for the city of Dundee. This £8 million project has been made possible through funding from:

Heritage Lottery Fund

Historic Scotland

The European Regional Development Fund

Dundee City Council

The McManus Galleries and Museum Fundraising Appeal is administered by Dundee Art Galleries and Museum Association Registered Charity (number sco17736). The project's honorary patrons are Lady Airlie, Brian Cox, Professor Sir Alfred Cuschieri, Lorraine Kelly, Professor Bernard King and Professor Geoff Ward. For further project information please visit www.mcmanus.co.uk.

opposite
Harry Keay, *Still Life with Lustre Jug*, 1941 [detail]

ACKNOWLEDGEMENTS

The National Galleries of Scotland and McManus Galleries and Museum, Dundee, are grateful to the following for their assistance with this publication and the associated exhibition: Neil Allan; Angela Bellany; John Bellany; Jeffrey Bertram, Wilhelmina Barns-Graham Charitable Trust; Chloë Blackburn; Amanda Brown; James Brown; Dennis Buchan; Val Cargill; Margaret Carlaw; Ruth Christie; Peter Collins; Dr Barbara Cowie; Professor Hilary Critchley; Dr Elizabeth Cumming; Senga Davidson, University of Dundee; Egan, Matthews and Rose Conservation; Olga Ferguson and Emily Hope Thomson, Aberdeen Art Gallery; Jim Fiddes, The Robert Gordon University Library, Aberdeen; John di Folco and Susan Keracher, Neil Dallas Brown Trust; Jane Furness, Scottish National Gallery of Modern Art; Carole Gibbons; Lynne Green; Douglas Hall; Jo Hall and Vicky Fieldgate, *Embroidery* magazine; Margaret Harrison, University of Strathclyde; John Houston; James Howie; Nicola Ireland and Joanna Soden, Royal Scottish Academy; Matthew Jarron, University of Dundee Museum Services; Robin Keay; Jack Knox; Ian Lamb and Angela Mathers, *The Courier*; Dr Margaret McCance; Robin McClure, The Scottish Gallery; Murdo MacDonald, Archivist, Argyll and Bute Council; Dr Siobhan MacHale; Joe McIntyre; James B.Mackellar; John McLean; Professor Will Maclean; Professor David Michie; James Morrison; Dr John Morrison; Laurence Morrocco; Alex Muir; William W. Payne, The Hospitalfield Trust; Guy Peploe, The Scottish Gallery; Lady Philipson; Dr John Ross; Dr Alastair Robertson Ross; Joseph Rhodes, Dunoon Grammar School; Hester Russell Grant, William Scott Archive; Robert Scott; Scottish Museums Council; Logan Sisley, Edinburgh College of Art; Dr Ian McKenzie Smith; Gavin Strang; Elspeth Sutton; Bill Taylor; Dave Taylor; Susannah Waters, Mackintosh Research Centre for Archives and Collections, Glasgow School of Art; Brenda Woods, Fine Art Library, Edinburgh.

Robert MacBryde, *Still Life,* 1959 [detail]

DUNDEE'S ART COLLECTION

The remarkable Gothic architecture of the McManus Galleries and Museum survives as a testament to nineteenth-century Dundee's confidence, wealth and intellectual ambition. Conceived as a focus for literature, science and art, designed by Sir George Gilbert Scott (1811–1878) and built entirely through private subscription, the building has been welcoming inquiring visitors since 1869.

Nineteenth-century Dundee was prosperous and the leaders of Dundee's business and professional communities were major civic patrons. A remarkable and dynamic group of individuals comprising industrialists, politicians and local gentry, they had energy, creativity and a passion for the arts. Privately they cultivated friendships with artists and established large art collections, and this private passion spilled over into the life of the city with the organisation of the hugely successful annual fine art exhibitions that ran from 1877 to 1891. The ambition of these shows was clearly demonstrated by the very first exhibition in 1877, which in size and scope was second only to London's Royal Academy exhibition of the same year. Importantly, these were *selling* exhibitions, featuring new work from the best of the British art establishment.

It was from these exhibitions in the last years of the nineteenth century that the city's nascent art collection began to grow. From the outset the collection was mainly a contemporary one, built through donations from individuals such as the engineer James Guthrie Orchar (1825–1898) and marmalade tycoon John Keiller (1851–1899). Orchar proved to be the art collection's major benefactor, presenting many works during his

own lifetime by his artist friends William McTaggart, John Pettie and George Paul Chalmers. His private collection – the only one to have survived intact – was transferred to the city's collection in 1987.

The permanent art collection grew through presentations and bequests until 1903 when John Morris (1819–1896), a local schoolteacher, bequeathed the huge sum of £3,000 to the Dundee Fine Art Association. Worth almost £250,000 in today's money, this was invested in government stocks and enabled the Fine Art Committee to select and purchase contemporary work. Through the Morris Trust Fund, the city acquired eighty paintings for the permanent art collection. Eight are featured here; including work by James Cowie, Ian Fleming, David McClure and Anne Redpath.

By 1917, the collection comprised over 350 paintings and was growing steadily enough for the first printed art catalogue of the collection to be published in 1926. Here the curator proudly proclaimed that not a single penny from Dundee Corporation had been spent on any of the paintings. The collection continued to build using private money. The modest Ower Bequest Fund was first used in 1932 and enabled the purchase of such gems as F.C.B. Cadell's *Still Life*, James McIntosh Patrick's *A City Garden* and S.J. Peploe's *Roses and Fan*.

In the 1940s a questionnaire was sent from Dundee to galleries across the UK asking if any of them collected 'abstract art' – obviously seen as very daring. There was considerable reluctance on the part of local authorities to purchase avant-garde art. We are grateful then for the

Alberto Morrocco, *Still Life on Red Cloth*, 1986 [detail]

work of the Contemporary Art Society, which presented the city with several notable works including Picasso-influenced paintings by Robert Colquhoun in 1959 and Robert MacBryde in 1962, and abstract works by Alan Davie in 1965 and William Scott in 1972. The CAS continues to support the gallery.

During the 1960s, a small annual sum from the council rates enabled the Gallery staff to actively collect work for the first time. Credit for this must go to our first curator, James D. Boyd, who was appointed in 1949. Previously the roles of chief librarian and curator were combined in one job. Since the 1960s it has also been possible to augment the funds available through the acquisition fund with government grant aid.

In 1968, the city's first keeper of art was appointed – the energetic and highly respected William R. Hardie, who held the post until 1976. For the first time since the collection was established, here was an individual who pursued a policy of buying progressive contemporary Scottish art. In his first year in post Hardie bought two recently completed paintings from gallerist Richard Demarco: Wilhelmina Barns-Graham's superb *Orange, Black and Lilac Squares on Vermilion* for £90 and Jack Knox's intriguing *Battle of San Romano II* for £50.

Hardie's most notable achievements, however, were in the area of early twentieth-century collecting. He contacted senior figures in Scottish art with a view to purchasing examples of their early experimental works. In 1975 from Stanley Cursiter, then aged eighty-eight, he bought the remarkable Futurist painting *Rain on Princes Street*, c.1913, for £1,000; and from

William Johnstone he bought the wonderfully surreal *Ode to the North Wind*, c.1929–31, for £700. These works, plus the splendid Vorticist *Mediterranean Hill Town*, 1923, by William McCance, filled important gaps in this area of the collection.

John Bellany's magnificent painting *The Lovers* was acquired in 1980 and heralded two decades of collecting the work of significant Scottish artists – especially those with a link to the Dundee area. Thus the focus here on John Duncan and James McIntosh Patrick, who is most closely associated with Dundee. Many of the artists featured, notably Alberto Morrocco, Will Maclean, Peter Collins and James Howie, have links with Dundee's outstanding art school.

There have been major changes in the arts infrastructure within Dundee over the last decade, not least the establishment of Dundee Contemporary Arts in 1999 and the emergence of the artist-run collective GENERATORprojects. Their presence has changed the artistic outlook of the city and has had a significant impact on the collection, encouraging the acquisition of work by artists of international renown (such as Anya Gallaccio, Catherine Yass and Roddy Buchanan) and a more systematic acquisition of work by emergent artists (including Robert Orchardson, Delia Baillie and Pernille Spence).

Two recent initiatives have supported these endeavours. We were fortunate to receive more than seventy works through the dispersal of the Scottish Arts Council's amazing collection in 1997. From the 1950s to the 1990s, independent panels of artists – rather than curators – had purchased innovative work for SAC. We received

fine work by Alexander Allan (featured here), established artists such as Mark Boyle, Bruce McLean, Steven Campbell and Adrian Wiszniewski, and work by the then emergent artists Callum Innes, Nathan Coley and Julie Roberts, now internationally acclaimed. More recently, we were one of six Scottish museums invited to participate in the new National Collecting Scheme for Scotland (NCSS) managed by the Contemporary Art Society with funds from the National Lottery via the Scottish Arts Council. Its first phase lasted from 2003 to 2006, during which time we purchased outstanding work by artists of international renown, such as Graham Fagen's bronze *Where the Heart Is*, Graeme Todd's painting *It is so endless* and Sophy Rickett's photographic triptych *Cypress Screen, Dundee*.

Dundee's art collection now comprises more than 6,500 items; the traditional media of painting, drawing, printmaking, and sculpture, have been joined by work from the new art disciplines of fine art photography and new media. We are optimistic for the future and sincerely hope that the collection continues as strongly throughout the twenty-first century as it has done through the last.

ANNA ROBERTSON and CLARA YOUNG
Art Curators, McManus Galleries and Museum

CATALOGUE

This publication features works by selected artists in Dundee's twentieth-century art collection, rather than being a comprehensive collection catalogue. It is a partial successor to W.R. Hardie, *Dundee City Art Gallery: Catalogue of the Permanent Collection of Paintings, Drawings and Sculpture*, Corporation of Dundee Museums and Art Galleries Department, 1973.

CATALOGUING NOTE

The information is presented in the following sequence:
— Artist's name
— Location and date of artist's birth and death or current living and working location
— Places and dates of main art education
— Places and dates of main teaching posts
— Places and dates of main non-teaching professional posts
— Membership of major art institutions, with Scottish institutions listed first
— Listing of all oils in order of accession, plus number of works on paper by each artist, in Dundee's collection
— Title and date – where a work has two titles the most commonly used comes first, the other follows in round brackets. Where the date is hyphenated, eg 1939–50, it means the artist worked on it during that period. Where the date is presented as 1939/50 it means the artist worked on it during those two years.
— Medium and dimensions, height × width × depth, in centimetres
— Credit line
— Museum number – which includes date of registration of the work into the collection

MCMANUS GALLERIES AND MUSEUM, DUNDEE

The Albert Institute of Science, Literature and Art was built between 1865 and 1869. An art galleries and museum wing opened in 1873, and the Victoria Art Galleries were added in 1889. For many years the building was variously referred to as Dundee Art Gallery, Dundee City Art Gallery or Dundee Museum. In 1984 the building was renamed after Dr Maurice McManus, who served two terms as Lord Provost of Dundee from 1960 to 1967, and is now known as McManus Galleries and Museum. The name Dundee Art Gallery is used throughout the text for the period up to 1984, except where exhibitions specifically publicised as being held in the Victoria Art Galleries are referred to, and as McManus Galleries and Museum thereafter.

DUNCAN OF JORDANSTONE COLLEGE OF ART AND DESIGN

Dundee College of Art originated in Dundee Technical Institute from the latter's founding in 1888, and its history as an art school dates from 1892. The name Dundee Technical College and School of Art was introduced in 1911, only to be changed to the Dundee Institute of Art and Technology in 1933. In 1953 a new art college building opened on Perth Road, which became known as Duncan of Jordanstone College of Art, although the name Dundee College of Art was also in use during the 1950s and 60s. The art college did not become an independent entity from the technical institution until 1975, but it became a faculty of the University of Dundee in 1994. In 1996 its name changed to Duncan of Jordanstone College of Art and Design, as it is now known. Where possible, the contemporary name, or name by which it would have been known by the artist referred to, has been used throughout the text.

NATIONAL FUND FOR ACQUISITIONS

Many works have been acquired with the help of the government's grant-aid scheme. This was originally called the Royal Scottish Museum grant, became the Local Museums Purchase Fund and is now called the National Fund for Acquisitions. All acquisitions made with assistance from the scheme are included in the credit line as an NFA grant.

ARTISTS

ALEXANDER ALLAN

Born Dundee 1914; died Dundee 1972

Studied Dundee College of Art 1932–6; Reimann School of Commercial and Industrial Art, London 1936–7; Westminster School of Art, London 1937–8; and Hospitalfield House, Arbroath, summer 1939

Taught Bell Baxter High School, Cupar 1952–61; Rockwell High School, Dundee 1961–8; and Duncan of Jordanstone College of Art, Dundee 1968–72

RSW

Fantastic Landscape, c.1938
Oil on board, 34 × 44.7
Scottish Arts Council Bequest 1997
1998–11

Plus two works on paper

Allan was born in Dundee in 1914 and studied there, in London and in Arbroath between 1932 and 1939. From 1940 until 1946 he worked for the Forestry Commission in Argyllshire before becoming an artist and teacher at schools in Fife and Dundee. He ended his career as a lecturer at Duncan of Jordanstone.

Allan is known as an exceptional draughtsman and painter of meticulously rendered landscapes, still lifes and portraits. His intensive working process involved observing his subject fastidiously and at length, before even making a mark on paper or canvas, eventually creating jewel-like images after months of careful consideration. As a result Allan was not very prolific, but he was still able to participate in the exhibitions of major art institutions, including the RSA, RA and RGI. From 1965 until his death he showed with the Glasgow Group, founded in 1958 to provide exhibiting opportunities for artists, becoming a member in 1968.

Fantastic Landscape dates from around 1938 and is thus a relatively early work in Allan's œuvre. Its precision and clarity show his sympathies with his teachers at Dundee, Edward Baird and James McIntosh Patrick and also with James Cowie, who was warden at Hospitalfield House when Allan studied there in 1939. The enigmatic still-life in the foreground, perhaps revealing an interest in Surrealism and Oriental art, is depicted in fine detail which, along with the brilliance of the red, contrasts with the softer technique used to create the atmospheric landscape in the background. This is based on a palette of carefully combined dark green and blue tones. The resulting image is at once beautiful, mysterious and sinister.

Allan travelled extensively in Europe throughout his career and a 1968 Scottish Arts Council Travel Award allowed him to work and study in Italy. His landscapes often recalled East Fife, Angus, north-west Scotland, Lake Lugano and Osteno. The artist Bill Taylor has commented on Allan's developing work: 'His later works – often small and displaying the influence of Georges Braque (1882–1963) – have a superficial simplicity and quiet beauty with exquisite colour and delicately poised compositions.'[1]

Allan had not established a widespread reputation by the time of his death in 1972, but is beginning to be recognised as an important modern Scottish artist. A memorial exhibition was mounted by Dundee Art Society in 1974, when *Fantastic Landscape* was purchased by the Scottish Arts Council, who presented it to McManus Galleries and Museum in 1997. A retrospective exhibition was held at Fair Maid's House Gallery, Perth, in 1986.

EDWARD BAIRD

Born Montrose 1904; died Montrose 1949
Studied Glasgow School of Art 1924–8
Taught Dundee College of Art 1938–40

Portrait of Walter Graham, *c.*1936
Oil on canvas, 92.1 × 71.7
Purchased 1968 from Mrs Ann Baird, the artist's widow
12a-1969

Plus one work on paper

Baird was born in Montrose and studied at Glasgow School of Art, where he became friends with James McIntosh Patrick. On graduating in 1927 he was awarded a travelling scholarship, which allowed him to work in Italy and to undertake post-graduate study. Early Italian Renaissance painting had a profound influence on Baird's work, which is characterised by extraordinary precision and clarity and involved a tortuously painstaking creative process. On his return from Italy in 1929 Baird returned to Montrose where he lived for the rest of his life.

The acute observation, classical approach and intellectual rigour of Baird's art reflect his independence from the expressive, painterly approach of so many of his Scottish contemporaries as well as the influence of James Cowie. Baird believed each part of his canvases to be of equal significance and continually re-worked his paintings. He rarely regarded them as finished, was loathe to sell them, and is thought to have produced no more than forty oils during his career. This strictly disciplined approach also related to Baird's socialist principles, believing that a picture should be the result of hard labour. As a Scottish Nationalist, the economic slump of the 1930s and resultant mass unemployment affected him profoundly. Baird's low level of productivity was also due to the serious ill-health from which he suffered throughout his life and which resulted in his death aged forty-five.

The subject of *Portrait of Walter Graham* is Baird's uncle, who was headmaster of Craig School, Ferryden, near Montrose. Following the early death of Baird's father, Graham became something of a mentor to the young man. He sat for the portrait in Baird's studio in Bridge Street and, as Patrick Elliott has commented:

> *The intensity of detail in the Graham portrait, particularly in the head, is remarkable ... Influenced by the technique of Flemish masters such as Jan van Eyck (fl. 1422–41), Baird would first paint with a monochrome under base and then layer it with glazes on top. If a white ground was used the paint could yellow with age and become transparent. This has happened in the foreground of the Graham portrait where the re-worked chess-pieces have almost disappeared, lending a ghostliness that does, unintentionally, complement the waxen and cadaverous head.*[2]

In 1942 Baird was appointed a war artist and executed a series of portrait drawings of Scottish munitions workers. In July 1944 ill-health forced him to go into hospital, where he remained until January 1945; shortly afterwards he married Ann Jeffrey Fairweather (1904–1972). He died in 1949 and a memorial exhibition was held at the Victoria Art Galleries, Dundee, the following year. The smallness of Baird's output, his ill-health, independent stance and spartan existence in a small Scottish town all contributed to his work being little known during his lifetime. However, his unique contribution to modern Scottish art is beginning to be recognised, as witnessed in retrospective exhibitions held at the Scottish National Gallery of Modern Art, Edinburgh, in 1992 and at The Fleming Collection, London, in 2004.

WILHELMINA BARNS-GRAHAM

Born St Andrews 1912; died St Andrews 2004
Studied Edinburgh College of Art 1931–7
Taught Leeds College of Art 1956–7
HRSA HRSW

Orange, Black and Lilac Squares on Vermilion, 1968
Oil and Cryla on hardboard, 76.8 × 76.8
Purchased 1968 with 50% NFA grant
9–1968

Plus three works on paper

Barns-Graham was born in St Andrews and studied at Edinburgh College of Art. She was an outstanding student, receiving several maintenance scholarships, vacation scholarships and a travelling scholarship, through which she remained linked to the college until 1942.

Due to her empathy for abstract art, the principal of ECA, Hubert Wellington, suggested Barns-Graham move to Cornwall in 1940, where a number of leading Modernist artists had gathered to escape war-time London. She stayed initially with the artist Margaret Mellis (b.1914) in Carbis Bay, near St Ives and through Mellis met Ben Nicholson (1894–1982), Barbara Hepworth (1903–1975) and Naum Gabo (1890–1977), amongst others. Inspired by their work and the surrounding sea and landscape, Barns-Graham became a leading member of the St Ives School, which came to the forefront of British art during the 1950s.

In 1960 Barns-Graham inherited the small Balmungo estate near St Andrews from her aunt and three years later bought a studio-residence in St Ives, overlooking Porthmeor Beach. These properties were to remain her bases for the rest of her life and symbolised her important dual roles in the development of Scottish and English art of the twentieth century.

Orange, Black and Lilac Squares on Vermilion is related to the *Things of a Kind in Order and Disorder* series which preoccupied the artist during the 1960s. These works explored cause and effect, colour theory and the interaction of simple geometric forms, essentially the square and the circle. Lynne Green, the artist's biographer, has explained about the series: '[The]

paintings were all essentially to do with interconnectedness, with the interdependency and inter-relatedness of life.'[3]

Orange, Black and Lilac Squares on Vermilion reveals Barns-Graham's acute sensitivity to colour and a kinship with the contemporary Op Art movement, with its emphasis on visual sensation. On seeing the work hanging at McManus Galleries and Museum in 2002, Barns-Graham told gallery staff that the changes in the colour sequence indicated the phrasing of the Lord's Prayer. Thus an orange or black square indicates a space and each lilac square a letter, so the first two 'lines' in the work relate to 'Our Father, Which Art in Heaven' and so on. Lynne Green has commented about the work: '[It] is one of a sequence of meditations on Barns-Graham's sense of the community of faith she found in the Church of England, not specifically related to her 1965 confirmation exactly, but to her sense of collectivity, of the shared experience, of belonging to the church.'[4]

Barns-Graham worked and exhibited prolifically throughout her long career, receiving great acclaim particularly towards the end of her life. Retrospectives and significant solo exhibitions were held in Edinburgh in 1989–90 at the City Art Centre; at the Scottish National Gallery of Modern Art in 1996–7; at the Crawford Arts Centre, St Andrews, in 2001; and Tate St Ives in 2000 and 2004. She was made a CBE for services to art in 2001 and died in St Andrews in 2004.

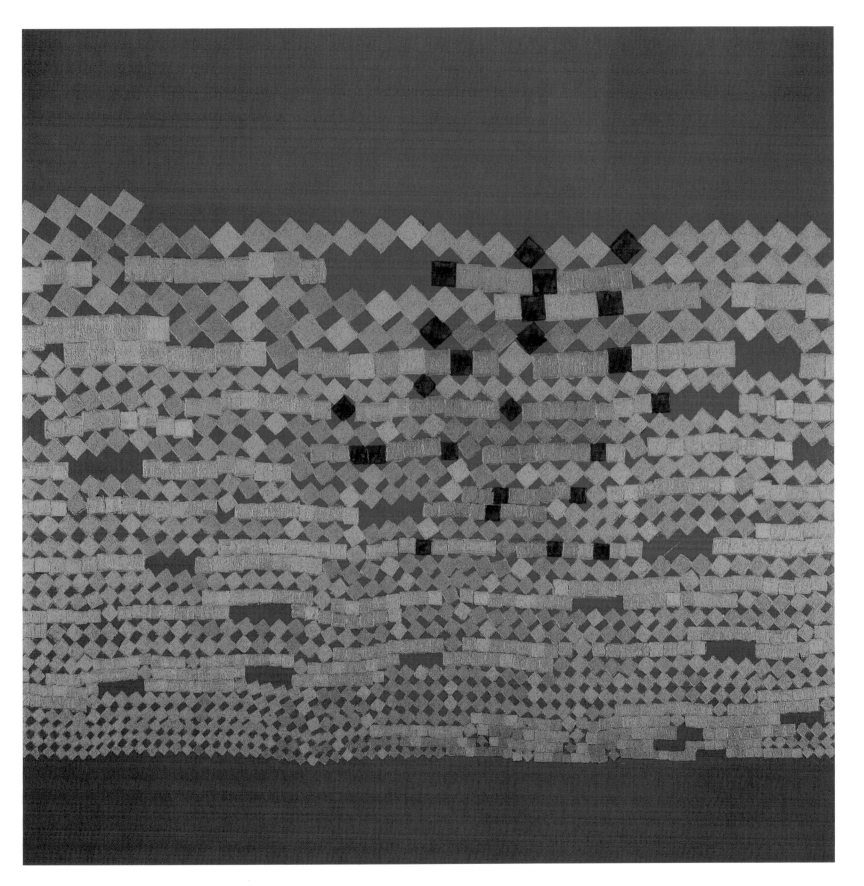

JOHN BELLANY

Born Port Seton 1942; lives and works Newport, Essex

Trained Edinburgh College of Art 1960–5 and Royal College of Art, London 1965–8

Taught Brighton College of Art 1968; Winchester College of Art 1969–73; Croydon College of Art, 1973–8; Goldsmith's College of Art, London; and Royal College of Art, London 1978–84

RA HRSA

The Lovers, 1979
Oil on canvas, 183.2 × 180.4
Purchased 1981 with 50% NFA grant
1–1981

Bellany was born in Port Seton, a fishing village on Scotland's east coast. His father and both grandfathers were fishermen. He attended Edinburgh College of Art, where he was taught by Robin Philipson. After graduating he studied at the Royal College of Art in London.

Bellany's upbringing in Port Seton's fishing community began to feature prominently in his work in the mid-1960s, by which time he had already established his interest in the concepts of life and death and of the sacred and the profane. In 1965 he saw a retrospective exhibition of the German artist Max Beckmann (1884–1950) at the Tate Gallery in London. The symbolic subject matter and deeply personal nature of Beckmann's œuvre came as a revelation. Two years later Bellany visited Buchenwald concentration camp, which shook his view of human nature to the core. As a result his work became darker and full of personal reference. He began to address issues such as death, guilt and sexual obsession through the symbols of fish, birds and other animals, sometimes fused with human figures. Bellany simultaneously developed a voluptuous palette of colours and a painting technique based on vigorous, expressive brushstrokes.

Bellany painted *The Lovers* in 1979 and it was included in the first *British Art Show*, which toured the UK that year. It features the artist with his second wife Juliet Lister (1939–1985), whom he married that year. Juliet suffered from ill-health and was to die six years later. This work comes from a series in which Bellany explored the complex emotional basis of their apparently doomed relationship. The lovers embrace intimately but also seem claustrophobically bound together. Bellany has disguised himself with a puffin's head, whilst Juliet is barely visible. They stand on the deck of the ship of life, behind the ship's wheel, which could be understood as a wheel of fortune. The sense of gambling, risk-taking and uncertainty is emphasised by the playing cards splayed out around the couple. The central image is framed by two strips on either side of the canvas, in which blurred images of former voyagers from life to death appear and dissolve into illegibility. Bellany has commented about *The Lovers*: 'This is a love poem in paint, and a tribute to the passion of love and the *tristesse* of lovers still bound together, when they are parting.'[5]

Bellany has had numerous solo exhibitions, such as those at the National Portrait Gallery in London in 1986 and retrospectives at the Scottish National Gallery of Modern Art in Edinburgh in 1986 and at the Hamburger Kunsthalle and Museum am Ostwall, Dortmund, in 1988–9.

DENNIS BUCHAN

Born Arbroath 1937; lives and works Arbroath

Studied Duncan of Jordanstone College of Art, Dundee 1954–9 and Hospitalfield House, Arbroath, summer 1959

Taught Duncan of Jordanstone College of Art, Dundee 1962–94

RSA

Above and Below the Blue, 1975
[ILLUSTRATED]
PVA and collage on canvas, 152 × 81
Scottish Arts Council Bequest 1997
1998–13

Music on a Rainy Day near the North Sea, 1994
Acrylic on canvas, 127 × 152.4
Purchased 1994 with 50% NFA grant
2000–42

Plus two works on paper

Buchan was born in Arbroath and studied at Duncan of Jordanstone College of Art, where he was encouraged to love rich colour by Alberto Morrocco, and at Hospitalfield House. For his National Service Buchan served with the Royal Army Education Corps from 1960 until 1962. Shortly afterwards he joined the staff of Duncan of Jordanstone, teaching alongside colleagues including Jack Knox, Peter Collins and David McClure. He remained there until his retirement in 1994.

In the 1960s Buchan was one of a group of young Scottish painters who embraced the possibilities offered by Abstract Expressionism, in particular its painterly freedom and un-fettered use of colour. Buchan had been working towards this approach independently and also found himself in sympathy with the work of the CoBrA artists, which he saw during visits to Amsterdam with his students during the 1960s and 1970s.

Buchan has remained loyal to an abstraction which retains a link to landscape elements of the Scottish north-east coast, and many of his works express his personal and sensuous experience of the North Sea. *Above and Below the Blue* was influenced by Buchan's then studio's proximity to Arbroath Harbour. Buchan resists overly literal interpretations of his images. In this painting he regards the blue as metaphorical rather than actual and as a space containing non-specific activity. A sense of a moment being captured, of contrasting speed and a medley of sounds is communicated, playing on the viewer's senses. The work is characteristic of Buchan's œuvre in its energy and dynamism,

seen both in his exuberant use of colour and in the spontaneity and generosity of his brush-strokes. The artist has commented:

> Above and Below the Blue *was part of a phase during which I used collage and expressionistic images, involving natural phenomena and man-made intrusions – clouds, sea, grids, aircraft etc. As such it was part of a series of works encom-passing these elements and creating reactions sometimes disturbing but primarily exciting forays into colour, media handling and image making … I still remember that period as a stimulating one.*[6]

Buchan is strongly associated with the arts in Dundee, not least because of his long-held and influential teaching position at Duncan of Jordanstone and his deeply felt connection with the environment, as experienced from his Arbroath base and expressed in his work. He was also included in two key exhibitions, *Five Dundee Painters* held at the Dundee Art Gallery in 1961 and *Seven Painters in Dundee* organised by the Scottish Arts Council, which toured throughout Scotland in 1972 and also featured Neil Dallas Brown, Peter Collins, Ian Fearn (b.1934), James Howie, James Morrison and Jack Knox. In 1961 Buchan became a member of the SSA. As a member of the RSA, he regularly shows work in their exhibitions and is represented by the Compass Gallery, Glasgow.

WILLIAM BURNS

Born Newton Mearns 1921; died Aberdeenshire 1972

Studied Glasgow School of Art 1944–8 and
Hospitalfield House, Arbroath, summers 1948 and
1949

Taught Dunoon Grammar School 1950–4; Ross High
School, Tranent 1954–5; and Aberdeen College of
Education 1955–70

RSA RSW

Seatown with Unterseeboot, 1965
Oil on board, 101.6 × 127
Purchased 1968 from the artist with 50% NFA grant
8–1968

Plus one work on paper

William Burns was born in Renfrewshire and served as a pilot in the Royal Air Force between 1939 and 1942. At one point he was stationed at Montrose, which introduced him to the Scottish east coast whose fishing towns and villages became an important source of inspiration. In 1944 he enrolled at Glasgow School of Art where he was taught by Ian Fleming. Burns graduated in 1948, the same year that Fleming was appointed warden of Hospitalfield House. As a result Burns studied there during the summers of 1948 and 1949.

After the war, Burns taught in Dunoon, Tranent and Aberdeen. In about 1958 he moved to the then small fishing village of Portlethen in Kincardineshire, to a cottage perched on a cliff, which overlooked the natural harbour below. In order to have a larger studio, he later purchased the former Craigie School and schoolhouse at Whitecairns, near Balmedie. During the late 1950s and early 1960s Burns flew a Tiger Moth, which he crash landed. However, he eventually renewed his pilot's licence, became a member of the Aberdeen and District Flying Club and acquired a Fournier light aircraft. As a result of his experiences flying, the naturalism of his early work gave way to boldly coloured images based on his emotional response to the local coastline and villages viewed from the sky. This can be seen in *Seatown with Unterseeboot* with its flattened, aerial perspective. 'Unterseeboot' means submarine in German.

Burns's works oscillate between dramatic, tactile, abstract surfaces in which confidently handled paint is applied with vigour, and evocative representations of the bustle of harbours battered by the raw forces of nature. As his friend, the architect Dave Taylor, has written: 'Bill matched the intense colours of the keels of the trawlers and composed abstract patterns out of harbour breakwaters with carefully placed propellers, funnels and boat shapes. However, it is the reality and feeling that is the essence of his work.'[7]

In 1955 Burns joined the staff of Aberdeen College of Education and was appointed principal lecturer in art in 1967. Dundee acquired *Seatown with Unterseeboot* the following year and Burns wrote to William Hardie, keeper of art, regarding the proposed purchase, commenting: 'I have hoped for a long time to have a representative work in Dundee Art Gallery.'[8] Burns resigned from his teaching post in 1970 in order to concentrate on painting. He died off the Kincardineshire coast on 14 October 1972 on a solo flight from Dundee to Aberdeen. A memorial exhibition was held at Aberdeen Art Gallery the following year, which toured to Glasgow and Edinburgh.

F.C.B. CADELL

Born Edinburgh 1883; died Edinburgh 1937

Studied Trustees' School of Art, Edinburgh c.1899 and
Académie Julian, Paris 1899–1902

RSA RSW

Still Life, c.1915
Oil on canvas, 63.5 × 76.2
Purchased 1932 with the Ower Bequest Fund
1–1932

The Farm, Dumfriesshire, c.1930
Oil on canvas, 63.5 × 76.2
Purchased 1957
41–1957

Iona, 1920s
Oil on canvas, 37.5 × 45
Bequeathed 1978 by Gordon Binnie
through The Art Fund
212–1978

Interior Regent Terrace, c.1932
Oil on canvas, 52 × 62
Bequeathed 1978 by Gordon Binnie
through The Art Fund
213–1978

Negro in White, c.1922
[ILLUSTRATED]
Oil on canvas, 76.2 × 63.8
Bequeathed 1978 by Gordon Binnie
through The Art Fund
214–1978

Along with John Duncan Fergusson, George Leslie Hunter and Samuel John Peploe, Francis Campbell Boileau Cadell is one of the four painters known as the Scottish Colourists, who are amongst the most celebrated of modern Scottish artists. He was born in Edinburgh and studied briefly at the Trustees' School of Art. In 1899 he moved to Paris and studied at the Académie Julian. He lived in Munich between 1906 and 1908. A visit to Venice in 1910 freed Cadell's technique and encouraged him to experiment with brighter colours. His work between then and the First World War was characterised by a lively impressionistic manner, as seen in Dundee's *Still Life* of around 1915.

Cadell spent most of the First World War in French trenches, returning to Edinburgh in 1919. During the 1920s he had a succession of stylishly decorated studios in the city's fashionable Georgian New Town. His surroundings and Edinburgh's polite society, of which he became a prominent member, became the subject matter of his work, which developed apace. A new intensity of colour, at times acidic, appeared, as did more structured and tightly defined compositions based on precise, flat brushwork which resulted in images verging on the abstract.

This approach can be seen in *Negro in White* which Cadell painted about 1922. The sitter was the boxer Mannie Abrew, who came from the nearby port of Leith and who sat for the artist on several occasions. His dark skin and strong physical presence made a change from the elegant society ladies who more regularly modelled for Cadell. The work was made in Cadell's drawing-room studio at 6 Ainslie Place.

The artist relished the contrast between Abrew's skin tones, the strong mauve colour with which he painted his studio wall and the bright whiteness of the boxer's vest. Flashes of brilliant colour are provided by the red chair and aspidistra, two of many such bold props with which Cadell animated his domestic surroundings and works.

Cadell exhibited regularly during his lifetime, often at Alexander Reid's gallery in Glasgow and with Aitken Dott & Son in Edinburgh, but he never achieved financial security. Deeply upset by the death of Peploe in 1935, Cadell died two years later. A retrospective of his work was held at the National Gallery of Scotland, Edinburgh, in 1942; a centenary exhibition was mounted at The Fine Art Society, London, in 1983.

Cadell exhibited with Fergusson, Peploe and Hunter on only three occasions whilst they were all alive. They showed as a foursome for the first time in Paris in 1924 and never constituted a formal group. The term 'Scottish Colourists' was first used as the title of an exhibition in 1948, when all but Fergusson had died. It was not until relatively recently that the term has come to be associated exclusively with these four artists.

ROBERT CARGILL

Born Arbroath 1940; died Arbroath 2001

Studied Duncan of Jordanstone College of Art, Dundee 1963–8

Taught Duncan of Jordanstone College of Art, Dundee 1968–70

Black Environment No. 4, 1967
PVA and collage on canvas, 106.7 × 106.7
Purchased 1970 from the artist
13–1969

Plus one work on paper

Cargill was born in Arbroath into one of the sea-town's oldest families. Whilst working as a compositor with *The Arbroath Herald*, he was allowed to use the facilities at Hospitalfield House. In 1963 he enrolled at Duncan of Jordanstone, where he later taught part-time.

Cargill is one of several artists who came to prominence in the second half of the twentieth-century, including James Morrison, Dennis Buchan and William Burns, who have drawn inspiration from the North Sea coastline from Dundee to Aberdeen. Cargill found himself in sympathy with the postwar Italian Arte Povera movement, in which poor quality, cast-off materials were used to question the aesthetics of fine art and the boundaries between painting and sculpture. Thus he would comb the local beaches and incorporate found objects, such as driftwood, in his works, using techniques such as collage and frottage to constantly challenge the understanding of what constitutes a 'painting'. Cargill used a limited palette of often somber colours, preferring a black ground and using broad, gestural forms to create a lively rhythm across the surfaces of his works. These deeply personal, abstract images paid homage to the way of life of his forebears and of North Sea fishermen and boatbuilders.

Black Environment No. 4 comes from a series of works for which Cargill won a Scottish Arts Council award in 1969 and about which he explained:

My black environment collage paintings are an involvement with nature in my native landscape. The land, the sea and the air and sometimes the element of time. I see the colours of the earth and the things that grow in it. I see the colours of the sky and the things that fly in it. I watch the water lapping and pounding on the rocks, the corrosion of the coast and the things cast up by the sea. These are the things I paint about.[9]

The artist's widow, Val Cargill, has explained about *Black Environment No. 4*:

The inspiration for most of his early paintings came from the north-east coast of Scotland. The hessian used on many of them was that which his father used to cover 'smokie' barrels, when smoking haddock in the traditional Arbroath way. This gave a rough effect on an often smooth black background. He embellished these with hiero-glyphic images … also with pieces of wood rope and so on, collected when searching the beaches around his home town.[10]

Cargill's challenging, non-figurative work received little official recognition during his lifetime. However, he exhibited frequently, including with the Richard Demarco Gallery and at the Talbot Rice Gallery, both in Edinburgh. Cargill moved to Majorca in 1994, where he was stimulated by the mountains and coastline, at once foreign but also connected to his surroundings in Arbroath, where he died in 2001.

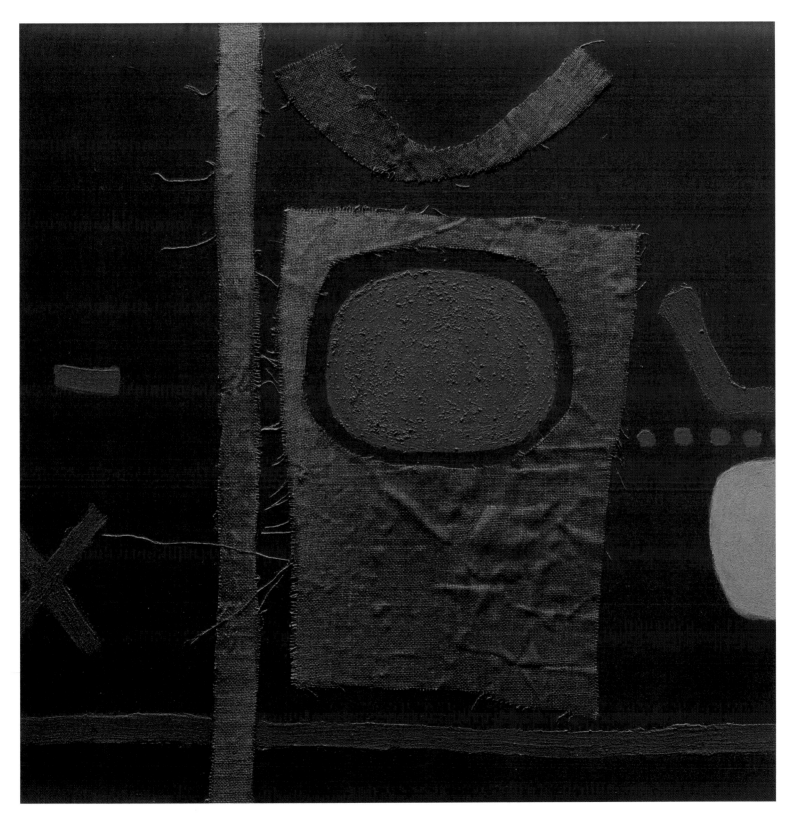

STEWART CARMICHAEL

Born Dundee 1867; died Dundee 1950
Studied Academy of Fine Arts, Antwerp 1888–91
Governor, Dundee College of Art 1936–50

Melita Resting (Millie Smeaton), 1921
Oil on canvas, 92.1 × 71.7
Presented 1920 by A. Sinclair Henderson
3–1920

Ex-Bailie Daniel Shoebotham Smith, J.P., 1926
Oil on canvas, 105.4 × 85.1
Presented 1926 by the sitter
12–1926

Self-portrait in the Artist's Studio, 1947
[ILLUSTRATED]
Oil on canvas, 51.1 × 61.2
Bequeathed 1951 by the artist
7–1973

The Meeting of St Kentigern and St Fergus, 1940
Oil on canvas, 134.6 × 101.6
Presented 1987, part of The Orchar Collection
272–1987–355

The Caravanner, c.1930
Oil on canvas, 63.5 × 50.8
Presented 1987, part of The Orchar Collection
272–1987–356

The Artist's Wife, c.1910
Oil on canvas, 76.2 × 49.5
Presented 1987, part of The Orchar Collection
272–1987–392

Mrs Jane Smith, 1924
Oil on canvas, 57.2 × 44.5
Presented 1987, part of The Orchar Collection
272–1987–397

Still Life (The Tanagra Figure), 1935
Oil on canvas, 50 × 41.2
Bequeathed 2001 by Mrs Freda Livie Bogie
2001–40

Plus seventy works on paper

Carmichael was born in Dundee. In 1883 he began to train as an architect at the office of James Hutton in Dundee, whilst attending evening art classes at the studio of Peter D. Lauder. Aged nineteen, he moved to London where he worked for the publishing firm Alexander Strachan & Co. Between 1888 and 1891 Carmichael travelled and studied in Antwerp, Brussels, Paris and Siena before returning to Dundee.

Carmichael was intensely interested in Scottish literature and history. This was reflected in much of his early work, which was influenced by the Symbolist movement of the late nineteenth century, whose aim was to resolve the conflict between the material and the spiritual world. He also played an important part in the Celtic Revival Movement, as did John Duncan. However, perhaps because of their greater commercial potential, by the 1920s local church architecture, landscape and portraiture began to occur more frequently in his œuvre.

Self-portrait in the Artist's Studio shows Carmichael's devotion to his native city. Painted in his city-centre studio in the Overgate, which he occupied for nearly forty years from 1910, it shows the young and old Carmichael against the backdrop of St Mary's Tower. Carmichael's flamboyant mode of dress is accredited to the time he spent in Paris and he preferred to wear a reefer jacket and generous bow tie with beret whilst working.

Carmichael exhibited extensively and internationally, including in Paris, Brussels, London, Edinburgh, Glasgow and Dundee. In 1896 he was elected a member of L'Aréopage, the Brussels art society. In 1905 he was a founding member of the exhibiting group the Tayport Artists' Circle, which also included David Foggie. He was a member of the Dundee Graphic Arts Association (which became Dundee Art Society in 1904) from 1890 and the Aberdeen Artists' Society from 1893 until 1935.

In 1905 Carmichael was appointed adviser for Higher drawings by the Scottish Education Department and he was governor of Dundee College of Art between 1936 and 1950. Carmichael was a well known and flamboyant figure in Dundee, where he died in 1950. A memorial exhibition was held in the Victoria Art Galleries the following year and the contents of his studio were bequeathed to Dundee Art Gallery. An important group of works was also presented to the Gallery in 1987 from The Orchar Gallery Collection, which was transferred in its entirety to McManus Galleries and Museum that year.

PETER COLLINS

Born Inverness 1935; lives and works Hilltown of Ballindean

Studied Edinburgh College of Art 1952–7

Taught Duncan of Jordanstone College of Art, Dundee 1965–93

RSA

The Sound of Silence, 1970
Oil on canvas, 127 × 101.6
Purchased 1970 with 50% NFA grant
2–1970

Consider the Lilies, 1971
[ILLUSTRATED]
Oil on canvas, 121.5 × 122
Scottish Arts Council Bequest 1997
1998–14

Collins was born in Inverness and studied at Edinburgh College of Art. His early paintings were figurative and characterised by a delicacy of line and sense of romanticism. In 1969, he turned to metaphysical realism as seen in *Consider the Lilies*.

Collins has explained the genesis and reasoning for this work:

Consider the Lilies is the second version of two paintings on the same theme and title … It was painted at a period when I was in thrall to American 'Magic Realism', which as a movement and a concept comes closer to the intensity of observation and hallucinatory poetry of a still life by the Spanish artist Francisco Zurbarán (1598–1664), than to surrealism.

The arum is a plant scorned in South Africa where it grows like a weed, yet for me it's the most beautiful of all the lilies in its pure sculptural form, albeit it is unabashedly phallic. I painted the flower and its yet unfurled neighbour employing a Victorian technique: painting into a not yet dried white ground, the pigments diluted with copal oil medium and applied very gently in minute strokes rendered with fine sable brushes. On the evidence, for example, of a painting by the Scottish artist John Faed (1819–1902) in the National Gallery of Scotland [The Evening Hour (Portrait Group of the Children of Dr Archibald Bennie), *c.1847*, NG 1142] *despite the passage of time this technique preserves a remarkable brilliance of tone.*

The cloth in the background was pinned and unpinned to and from my studio wall during many hours of trial and error, until the folds were arranged to my satisfaction. There is an implicit and intended association with St Veronica's veil, despite the absence of an imprint of Christ's head.

Rather than the white walls of my studio, I invented the dark void beyond. All is contained within a 'viewfinder'. To ensure that the shadows of this frame were correct, I constructed from grey mounting card, on a much smaller scale, the painting's visual gateway.

Classical music is one of the sustaining joys of my life and I subscribe to the belief that 'painting aspires to the condition of music.' Music is an abstract art, and though 'Realist' could be an apt label for Consider the Lilies *I hope that my explanation does not destroy the magic of a creation, where in its composition and orchestration there is much instinct and abstract thought. I prefer my butterflies not to be pinned to a board!*[11]

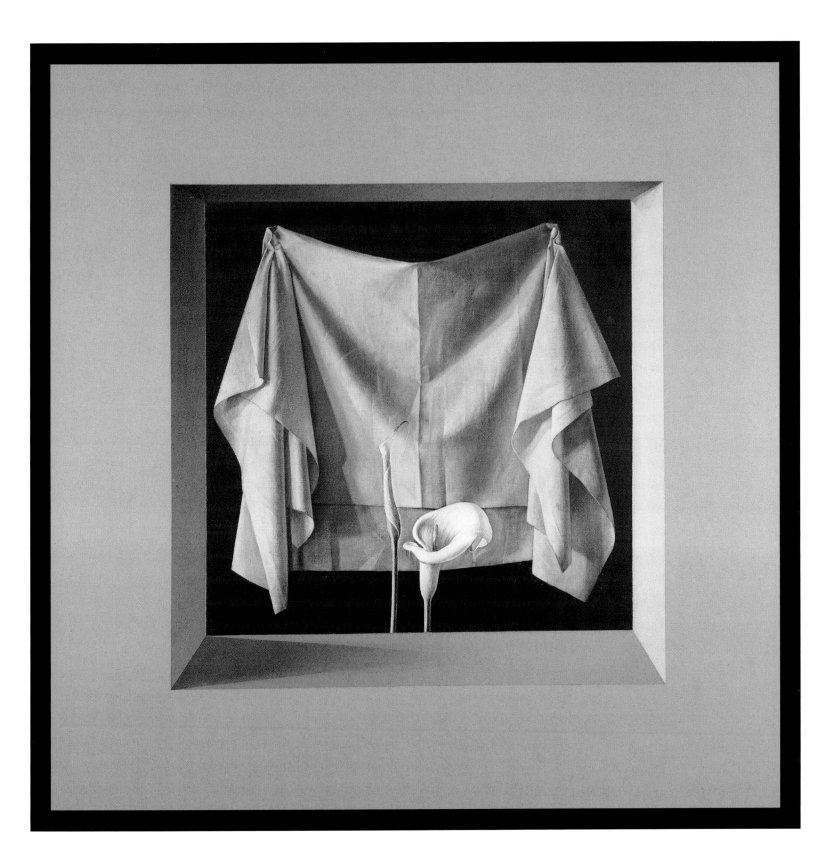

ROBERT COLQUHOUN

Born Kilmarnock 1914; died London 1962

Studied Glasgow School of Art 1932–8; Hospitalfield
House, Arbroath, summer 1938; and Jordanhill
Teacher Training College, Glasgow 1939–40

Woman by a Leaded Window, 1958
[ILLUSTRATED]
Oil on canvas, 91.4 × 71.4
Presented 1959 by the Contemporary Art Society
16–1959

Young Man in a Landscape (David Haughton), 1943
Oil on canvas, 60 × 76.5
Purchased 1978 with 45% NFA grant
215–1978

Colquhoun was born in Kilmarnock, Ayrshire, not far from Maybole where Robert MacBryde was born and with whom Colquhoun is inextricably linked. They met at Glasgow School of Art and lived and worked together for the rest of Colquhoun's life. 'The two Roberts', as they were known, graduated in 1938 and spent that summer at Hospitalfield House where James Cowie was warden. Travelling scholarships enabled them to study in France and Italy. On their return to Scotland Colquhoun trained as a teacher and in 1940 he joined the Royal Army Medical Corps in Edinburgh. He was invalided out the following year, after which the Roberts moved to London. They shared a studio with the painter John Minton (1917–1957) and became associated with the contemporary neo-Romantic movement, but their experience of avant-garde French art meant that their work was also inspired by Pablo Picasso (1881–1973) and Georges Braque (1882–1963) as well as by the English modernist Wyndham Lewis (1882–1957).

In 1943 the Polish artist Jankel Adler (1895–1949) moved to a studio in their building. Adler encouraged Colquhoun to paint from imagination and experience rather than from a model. He also inspired the younger artist to turn from landscape painting to concentrate on the figure, often set within a shallow picture space as seen in *Woman by a Leaded Window*. This painting is typical of the brightly coloured, geometrically stylised approach of Colquhoun's later years, in which his pared down compositions and schematised figures were outlined with black and painted in a flat, unemotional manner.

Colquhoun had his first solo exhibition in

1943, at the Lefevre Gallery in London. It was a success and Colquhoun was fêted by the English art world. However, by the mid-1940s Colquhoun had arguably reached the peak of his creative powers and reputation; thereafter ill-health and hard living resulted in a gradual decrease in his productivity and originality.

The two Roberts made names for themselves as theatre designers in the latter part of their careers. In 1948 they were commissioned by the Russian choreographer Léonide Massine (1895–1979) to design the décor and costumes for a new Scottish ballet, *Donald of the Burthens*, which premiered at Convent Garden in 1951. They also designed the costumes and sets for George Devine's production of *King Lear* at Stratford in 1953.

A retrospective exhibition at the Whitechapel Art Gallery, London, in 1958 spurred Colquhoun to make new work but it was not well received and he concentrated on drawing and monotypes thereafter. He died in 1962. Memorial exhibitions were held in Edinburgh and Kilmarnock and a retrospective toured Scotland in 1981. A joint retrospective of Colquhoun and MacBryde's work was mounted at Glasgow Print Studio in 1990.

JAMES COWIE

Born Cuminestown, Aberdeenshire 1886;
died Edinburgh 1956

Studied Aberdeen University and United Free Training
College, Aberdeen 1906–9 and Glasgow School of Art
1912–14

Taught Fraserburgh Academy, 1909–12; Bellshill
Academy, 1915–16 and 1918–35; and Gray's School of
Art, Aberdeen 1935–7

Warden, Hospitalfield House, Arbroath 1937–48

RSA

Portrait of a Child, 1948
Oil on canvas, 101.9 × 68.9
Purchased 1951 from the artist with the
Morris Trust Fund
12–1951

Plus one work on paper

Cowie was born in Aberdeenshire and in 1906 he began to study English at Aberdeen University whilst training to be a teacher at the city's United Free Training College. On qualifying in 1909 Cowie became art master at Fraserburgh Academy and by 1912 had saved enough money to study at Glasgow School of Art, where he completed the Diploma course in just two years. In 1915 Cowie was appointed to teach at Bellshill Academy, where he remained until 1935 except for two years spent as a conscientious objector during the First World War. He then taught for two sessions at Gray's School of Art, Aberdeen.

Cowie painted *Portrait of a Child* in Edinburgh in 1948. It is based on an earlier work, *Miss Barbara Graham Cowie*, of 1938–9 (oil on plywood, RSA Diploma Collection, 2000.088) which he made whilst warden of Hospitalfield House. Both works depict his younger daughter Barbara (b.1930) and show Cowie's independent stance as a twentieth-century Scottish artist, in which he rejected colourful, expressive painterly qualities for an intellectual, classical approach based on drawing, tone, architectonic characteristics and a painstakingly slow working process. Their complex composition – presenting the sitter in a room, within a painted oval frame over which Barbara's foot and the draped material extend – relates to Cowie's interest in the Surrealist work of the English painter Paul Nash (1889–1946) and in the exaggerated perspective of Italian Quattrocento artists, such as Carlo Crivelli (c.1430–1495) and Andrea Mantegna (1431–1506). The chair on which the material is draped, and on which an open book rests, acts as a link between the foreground and background

of the paintings. In both, the artist's daughter is depicted in a dignified, full-length frontal pose, reaching her arm across her chest to her neck, at the centre of complex inter-relationships with the still-life objects. Cowie presented the earlier work to the Royal Scottish Academy Diploma Collection following his election as an academician in 1943.

Cowie's first solo exhibition was held at the McLellan Galleries, Glasgow, in 1935. His next was mounted by the Arbroath Art Society in 1947 and travelled in smaller form to T. & R. Annan & Sons in Glasgow. His third and final solo show held during his lifetime was at The French Institute, Edinburgh, in 1951. Cowie exhibited regularly with the RSA and at the RGI and through his teaching positions wielded considerable influence on the development of modern Scottish art, seen for example in the importance of linear clarity in the work of Robert Colquhoun and Robert MacBryde, who studied under him at Hospitalfield House. Cowie died in 1956 and the following year the Arts Council Scottish Committee organised a memorial exhibition which toured six venues in Scotland. Retrospective exhibitions have since been organised by the Fine Art Society, London, in 1976, at the Scottish National Gallery of Modern Art, Edinburgh, in 1978 and the Scottish Arts Council in 1981–2.

HUGH ADAM CRAWFORD

Born Busby, East Renfrewshire 1898; died
Blanefield 1982

Studied Glasgow School of Art 1919–23; Central
School of Arts and Crafts, London; and St Martin's
School of Art, London 1924–5

Taught Glasgow School of Art 1925–48; Gray's School
of Art, Aberdeen 1948–53; and Dundee College of Art
1954–64

RSA

Washing by the River (Broughty Ferry, Dundee), 1958
[ILLUSTRATED]
Oil on canvas, 76.2 × 101.6
Purchased 1958 with the Morris Trust Fund
18–1958

William Hughes, Lord Provost of Dundee 1954–60,
1961
Oil on canvas, 127 × 101.6
Presentation portrait 1961
1971–24

Hugh Adam Crawford was born in Busby and
grew up in Garelochhead. He worked in a stained
glass and metalwork studio before joining the art
department of the *Glasgow Herald*. Aged seven-
teen, he joined the Royal Field Artillery. He
returned to Glasgow in 1919 and won a scholarship to study at Glasgow School of Art. After
graduating he studied in London before joining
the staff of Glasgow School of Art in 1925. He was
head of drawing and painting from 1938 until
1948 when he became head of Gray's School of
Art in Aberdeen. In 1954 Crawford became
principal of Dundee College of Art, where he
remained until retirement in 1964.

Crawford is affectionately remembered by
former colleagues and students alike as an
outstanding art teacher. Amongst his particular
protégés, who went on to become significant
artists, were Robert Henderson Blyth (1919–
1970), Joan Eardley (1921–1963) and Robert
Colquhoun. Crawford's professional responsibilities limited the amount of time he could
dedicate to his own painting. With typical
modesty he admitted:

> The reason why I am not a good painter in the
> way I wanted to be a good painter is partly
> because I was never able to resist the idea of a
> group of students being like a garden – some need
> weeding and others need a load of dung ... What I
> enjoyed as much as anything was the diversity of
> personality.[12]

Nevertheless, Crawford produced a sizeable
body of work. During the 1930s he established a
life-long reputation as a portraitist. He received
numerous official and private commissions,
amongst them that to paint William Hughes,

Lord Provost of Dundee from 1954 until 1960.
This portrait is now in Dundee's collection. He
also painted significant murals, including those
for the Roman Catholic chapel at Bellahouston
and in the church on the exhibition site of the
1938 Glasgow Empire exhibition.

Crawford painted *Washing by the River
(Broughty Ferry, Dundee)* whilst living in
Broughty Ferry. The bright, almost abstract
forms of the white washing are blown by a
hearty wind which does not seem to affect the
fisherman working on the shore. The washing,
bollards and frame provided by the harbour wall
and building on the right create a strong composition. The subtle palette of blues, greens and
greys conveys not only Crawford's sensuous
feeling for paint but also the blustery weather
and light of the north-east coast. Crawford's
former student, the sculptor Alastair Robertson
Ross, has recalled how Crawford mixed his
paints on a pane of glass laid on a piece of white
paper, believing this resulted in more accurate
colours than those mixed on a dark mahogany
palette, as they were to be applied to a white
canvas.[13]

Crawford regularly exhibited with the Dundee
Art Society, as well as at the RGI and RSA and
with the SSA. Crawford had solo exhibitions at
the RGI and Scottish Gallery, Edinburgh, in 1934.
Almost forty years passed before the next, a
retrospective held at the Glasgow Art Club in
1971. Following his retirement, Crawford moved
to Blanefield, near Glasgow, where he enjoyed a
flush of creative activity before his death in 1982.

STANLEY CURSITER

Born Kirkwall 1887; died Stromness 1976
Studied Edinburgh College of Art 1904–8
Director, National Galleries of Scotland 1930–48
King's Painter and Limner in Scotland 1948–76
RSA RSW

Orkney Landscape, 1952
Oil on canvas, 50.8 × 61
Purchased 1956
33–1956

Rain on Princes Street, c.1913
[ILLUSTRATED]
Oil on canvas, 51.4 × 61
Purchased 1975 from the artist with 50% NFA grant
1–1975

Cursiter was born in Kirkwall, Orkney. He served an apprenticeship as a chromolithographic designer while attending evening classes at Edinburgh College of Art. He became a full-time student at the college in 1908 and established himself as a designer and painter the year after. He became enthusiastic about Post-Impressionism and Futurism, then at the cutting-edge of modern art, having seen them in London exhibitions.

Rain on Princes Street is one of a series of seven paintings, all of 1913, inspired by the Italian Futurists, making Cursiter one of the very first artists in Britain to explore their ideas. Led by the poet Filippo Marinetti (1876–1944), the Futurists glorified the modern world, machinery, movement and speed, as seen in the paintings of Gino Severini (1883–1966) and Umberto Boccioni (1882–1916). In *Rain on Princes Street* Cursiter stylised the figures, umbrellas and architectural features of the main thoroughfare in Edinburgh's New Town, to convey the street's wet, crowded and bustling atmosphere.

The lamp standards were replaced during World War One, shortly after Cursiter had painted them. The two with figures stood at the edge of the pavement outside the Life Association Building at 81–3 Princes Street which was demolished in 1970 and replaced by shops. The other lamp standards are those of the New Club at 85 Princes Street, which was demolished and re-built in the late 1960s. The squares on the right-hand side of the picture are the half-blocked columns of the entrance to the Life Association. The striped section recalls the sun blind of the shop in the western half of its

ground floor. The features on the left-hand side of the image are thought to relate to the tramcars which ran along the south side of the street.[14]

Dundee purchased *Rain on Princes Street* from the artist in 1975, some sixty years after it was painted. Cursiter wrote to William Hardie, keeper of art: 'I am so pleased that you are interested in these early works, I have always kept them as I thought they had something to say. All my later work was of a more conventional character – I became a portrait painter more or less by accident.'[15]

At the outbreak of World War One, Cursiter joined the 1st Battalion of the Scottish Rifles and was demobilised in 1919. He never returned to working in the Futurist style, but became a celebrated portraitist, landscape painter and lithographer. Between 1930 and 1948 he was director of the National Galleries of Scotland. In 1948 he was appointed King's Painter and Limner in Scotland and retired from the Galleries to his native Orkney. There he devoted himself to landscape painting and recording Orcadian life. He died in Stromness in 1976.

NEIL DALLAS BROWN

Born Elgin 1938; died St Andrews 2003

Studied Duncan of Jordanstone College of Art, Dundee 1954–9; Hospitalfield House, Arbroath, summer 1958; and Royal Academy Schools, London 1960–1

Taught Duncan of Jordanstone College of Art, Dundee 1968–79 and Glasgow School of Art 1979–98

Fallen Image, c.1964
Oil on canvas, 127 × 127
Purchased 1965 with the Morris Trust Fund
2–1965

Fairy Tale or Summer Incident, 1966
[ILLUSTRATED]
Oil on board, 96.5 × 121.9
Presented 1972 by the artist
25–1972

Meadow (Thunderclap), c.1987
Oil on hardboard, 91.5 × 60.5
Presented 2006 by Neil Dallas Brown Trust
2006–13

Protector (Coast), c.1997
Mixed media, 33 × 60.7 × 15.5
Presented 2006 by Neil Dallas Brown Trust
2006–14

Fluttering Rag (Ulster Dawn), 1981
Oil on canvas, 184.5 × 185
Presented 2006 by Neil Dallas Brown Trust
2006–15

Majestic Sea Brooder (For the Wild Bird), 1994
Oil, sand and acrylic gel on panel, 192 × 33
Presented 2006 by Neil Dallas Brown Trust
2006–16

Woman and Cat in Apartment, 1971
Oil on board, 100.5 × 161.5
Presented 2006 by Neil Dallas Brown Trust
2006–17

Dallas Brown was born in Elgin and studied at Duncan of Jordanstone and the Royal Academy Schools in London. He won several prestigious academic scholarships, travelling scholarships and awards, the latter allowing him to work in France, Italy and Spain from 1959 until 1960 and New York in 1967. In 1970 he was the major prize winner at the Arts Council of Northern Ireland Open Painting Exhibition. His first solo exhibition was held at the Duncan Institute, Cupar, in 1959, a retrospective exhibition of his work toured Britain in 1975 and an exhibition of his shaped paintings and constructions was shown in Dundee and Pittenweem in 2001.

As an imaginative figurative and abstract landscape painter and as a teacher in Dundee and Glasgow for thirty years, Dallas Brown exerted considerable influence on the course of modern Scottish art. He painted *Fairy Tale or Summer Incident* on six separate boards in 1966. Its apocalyptic feel, surrealist overtones and enigmatic imagery are painted with masterly technique in a palette of sombre greens and browns. The viewer is left to puzzle over what the 'Fairy Tale' or 'Summer Incident' could be.

In 1966 Dallas Brown wrote in his journal:
For many years ... the basic images in my work have evolved through the progressive interest in the relationship of figures themselves in an exterior setting, the theme strongly rooted in a romantic realism ... The interest in the interpretation of emotions through landscape forms has rapidly increased between 1960 and 1966 ... After six years on the same theme the path that I have followed has come to a fork and I have explored by certain tentative feelers both of the possible routes which I must now take ... The one path leads to an increasingly powerful realism concerning variations of a constant theme of impersonal elemental heads and shoulders in landscape and the other path goes off in the direction of exploration of mood created by a subjective distortion of physical form landscape ... The crystallisation of an image in my mind is like a new discovery every time for me. A heavy burden which has been working on me unloaded.[16]

Dallas Brown's reputation was secured by a body of work made in the late 1960s and 1970s in response to sectarian violence in Northern Ireland, known as the 'Ulster Series' or 'Shroud Paintings'. He lived in Fife's East Neuk for many years and in his later work he turned to shaped and padded canvases to reflect the interplay between the sea, shoreline and man-made structures in his surroundings. Dallas Brown died in St Andrews in 2003. Two years later a trust was formed in order to disperse works from his estate to public collections throughout Scotland.

JOHN DUNCAN

Born Dundee 1866; died Edinburgh 1945

Studied Academy of Fine Arts, Antwerp 1889–90

Director, Old Edinburgh Art School 1893–7

Taught School of Education, Chicago University 1900–3 and Royal Scottish Academy School of Painting, Edinburgh 1919–22

RSA

The Riders of the Sidhe, 1911
[ILLUSTRATED]
Tempera on canvas on board, 114.3 × 175.2
Presented 1912 by Mr J. Martin White
178–1912

The Children of Lir, c.1914
[ILLUSTRATED]
Tempera on canvas, 61 × 50.8
Purchased 1924 with the Morris Trust Fund
18–1924

The Play Garden, 1913
[ILLUSTRATED]
Tempera on canvas, 121.9 × 182.8
Purchased 1942 with the Morris Trust Fund
11–1942

The Fomor (The Powers of Evil Abroad in the World), 1939
Tempera on canvas, 101.6 × 152.4
Presented 1946 by the artist's trustees
4–1945

Peacocks and Fountain, 1905
Tempera on canvas, 54.6 × 121.9
Bequeathed 1951 by Miss Margaret Jane Cunningham
10–1951

Portrait of a Lady, c.1900
Oil on canvas, 43.2 × 33
Presented 1987, part of The Orchar Collection
273–1987–10

The Unicorns, 1920
Tempera on canvas, 35.3 × 68.5
Bequeathed 1966 by Mrs Deirdre Inches Carr, Edinburgh
2000–63–1

Plus twenty-six works on paper

Duncan was born in Dundee and is one of the most distinguished artists to be associated with the city. Between the ages of thirteen and twenty he produced several etchings and drew illustrations for local papers including *The Wizard of the North*. After three years as a book illustrator in London, he enrolled at the Academy of Fine Arts in Antwerp in 1889, under Charles Michael Maria Verlat (1824–1890). Before his return to Dundee the following year, he travelled to Italy, where he was inspired by the work of early Italian Renaissance painters.

Duncan is renowned as the foremost painter of the late nineteenth-century Celtic Revival movement, led by the sociologist and botanist Patrick Geddes (1854–1932). The movement aimed to evoke a pre-British Scotland and to stress Scotland's individual cultural identity. Encouraged by Geddes, whom he met in 1891, Duncan began to depict imaginative recreations of Gaelic myths, legends and historical events. He became intimately involved with Geddes's Edinburgh-based projects, for example becoming the main illustrator of the quarterly publication *The Evergreen*, creating murals for Ramsay Lodge where Geddes lived, and acting as director of the Old Edinburgh School from 1893 until 1897.

In 1903 Duncan returned to Scotland after three years teaching in Chicago. He settled in Edinburgh and over the next fifteen years created some of his most celebrated paintings, including *The Riders of the Sidhe*. He painted this with egg tempera, with which he had begun to experiment in 1910 and which became his preferred medium. The inscription on its frame reads: 'The Riders of the Sidhe, Lords of Life, bearing as symbols the Tree of Experience, The Love-Cup, The Sword of Will, and the Stone of Quietness.' In Celtic myth the Sidhe (pronounced Shee) are Celtic fairy folk. Each year on Midsummer Night they ride forth to a sacred circle to initiate mortals into the mysteries of their faith.

Duncan explained the meaning of this work: *Each rider carries a symbol of age-long Celtic tradition. The Tree of Life means wisdom. The Love-Cup, the Grail cup of the heart of abundance and healing, is the symbol of Love. The Sword is the symbol of power or the will in action. The Stone of Quietness is the symbol of the will in its passive form, the crystal that reveals the past and the future.*[17]

The designs of the armour and other trappings are inspired by ancient Celtic metalwork. For example, the shield is similar to the Iron Age Battersea Shield of 350BC in the British Museum, London (P&EE 1857.7–15.1). Much of the imagery in the painting was inspired by Pictish symbol stones which Duncan saw in Dundee and Edinburgh. The swastika on the horse's harness is an ancient symbol of life, sun, strength and good luck. *The Riders of the Sidhe* was exhibited at the Royal Scottish Academy in 1911 where it was purchased by J. Martin White. White knew Duncan through Geddes, whose chair of botany at University College, Dundee, he endowed, and he presented the painting to the city in 1912.

In contrast *The Play Garden* of 1913 is more light-hearted and was originally called *Child's Garden*. The crowded composition contains tableaux of children enjoying activities from sailing, digging and dressing-up to playing with

The Play Garden, 1913

The Riders of the Sidhe, 1911

animals, whilst their modern-day costume heightens the sense of achievable fantasy. Scenes from children's books, fairy stories and nursery rhymes abound, including *Sinbad the Sailor*, *The Little Mermaid*, *Alice's Adventures in Wonderland*, *Kim and the Elephant* and *I'm the King of the Castle*. The border of the canvas is ornamented by little grotesque animals. Duncan's daughter Christine (b.1914) remembers how he used to entertain her and her sister Vivian (b.1915) with his funny drawings.

Dundee's *The Children of Lir*, *c*.1914 is a smaller version of an earlier work in the collection of City of Edinburgh Museums and Art Galleries (CAC 292.1964). Lir was a mythical Celtic god. Made jealous by his love for his children, their step-mother Aiofe transformed them into swans, doomed to wander lakes and seas for 900 years. Duncan brings Celtic ornament into his picture in the form of amulets about the necks of the swan, girl and kneeling boy. The children, set against a background of a stormy sea, were modelled on those of Dr Otto Schlapp, lecturer in German and Teutonic philology at Edinburgh University.

Duncan became a leading figure in first the Dundee and then the Edinburgh art scenes. In Dundee his circle of friends included George Dutch Davidson (1879–1901), with whom Duncan briefly shared his studio in 1898–9, and Stewart Carmichael. Both owed much to Duncan, and the latter's interest in mystical and romantic themes helped to ensure the survival of Celtic Revivalism into the 1940s. Duncan exerted a huge influence on the Scottish Symbol- ist and decorative tradition centred around Edinburgh and encouraged the early work of artists such as Stanley Cursiter and Cecile Walton (1891–1956). In the latter part of his career Duncan received several religious commissions, including those for stained-glass designs as seen in the *Creation* window in North Morningside Church in Edinburgh and the Coates Memorial Window in Paisley Abbey. In 1941 a retrospective exhibition, an unprec- edented honour for a living artist, was held at the National Gallery of Scotland, Edinburgh. After Duncan's death in 1945, his trustees distributed his most significant paintings amongst Scottish museums.

The Children of Lir, *c*.1914

JOHN DUNCAN FERGUSSON

Born Leith 1874; died Glasgow 1961
RBA

Joan, 1916
Oil on card, 34.9 × 27.3
Presented 1956 by the Contemporary Art Society
25–1956

Full of the Warm South, 1953
Oil on canvas, 77.5 × 64.7
Purchased 1968 from the J.D. Fergusson Foundation
with 50% NFA grant
11–1962

A Lowland Church, 1916
[ILLUSTRATED]
Oil on canvas, 50.8 × 55.9
Purchased 1968 from the J.D. Fergusson Foundation
with 50% NFA grant
12–1962

Fergusson is one of the four artists known collectively as the Scottish Colourists. The others are Francis Campbell Boileau Cadell, George Leslie Hunter and Samuel John Peploe. Fergusson was born in Leith and, apart from short-term enrollments at painting academies in Edinburgh and Paris, was self-taught. His first trip to Paris, then the undisputed capital of the art world, is thought to have been in 1897. He returned repeatedly, sometimes with Peploe with whom he painted in the south and northwest of France, before moving to Paris in 1907. He soon became intimately involved with the avant-garde scene and began exhibiting at the Salon d'Automne that year. More than any of his Scottish contemporaries, Fergusson assimilated and developed the latest developments in French painting.

In 1913 Fergusson met the dancer Margaret Morris (1891–1980) who became his life-long partner and they moved to the Cap d'Antibes, where she established a modern dance school. On the outbreak of the war the couple moved to London where the Margaret Morris Club became an important gathering place for local artists, writers and composers.

During the summers of 1915 and 1917 Fergusson spent extended periods with his family in Bonnyrigg on the outskirts of Edinburgh. In 1914 he had painted a watercolour of nearby Lasswade Parish Church (The Fergusson Gallery, Perth, 1992.345) from which he developed *A Lowland Church* in 1916. The distinctive building, which was demolished in 1955, was originally designed by Robert Adam (1728–1792) but was constructed by his brother-in-law John Clerk (1722–1812). The schematic design of the painting, the illusion of volume, particularly in the trees and the hatched brushstrokes, recall the work of Paul Cézanne (1839–1906), as well as Fergusson's love of voluptuous form and rhythmic contours. The rainbow colours in the clouds are reminiscent of the highly coloured Orphism of Robert Delaunay (1885–1941), which developed in Paris from 1909 to 1912.

After the Second World War, Fergusson and Morris spent increasing amounts of time in Paris and the south of France. Fergusson continued to exhibit in Paris, London, Glasgow and elsewhere in Scotland, sometimes in the company of Cadell, Hunter and Peploe. In 1937 Fergusson became president of Le Groupe d'Artistes Anglo-Américains but was forced to leave Paris for London in 1939 at the outbreak of the Second World War. The following year he and Morris moved to Glasgow where they galvanised the arts scene, being founder members of the New Art Club – a meeting and exhibiting society – and its off-shoot the New Scottish Group. During the 1950s the couple spent long periods in the south of France, where Morris's creative dance movements and the students at her Summer Schools became Fergusson's favourite models.

Fergusson died in 1961, twenty-four years later than Cadell, the longest-lived of the other Colourists. A memorial exhibition was held that year at the RSA (which subsequently toured Scotland and travelled to Eastbourne) and in 1963 the J.D. Fergusson Art Foundation was formed by Margaret Morris to administer the artist's estate, from whom Dundee purchased *A Lowland Church* and *Full of the Warm South*. In 1991 The Fergusson Gallery, Perth, was established with a gift of holdings from the Foundation.

IAN FLEMING

Born Glasgow 1906; died Aberdeen 1994

Studied Glasgow School of Art 1924–9 and Jordanhill Teacher Training College, Glasgow 1930–1

Taught Glasgow School of Art 1931–48 and Gray's School of Art, Aberdeen 1954–72

Warden, Hospitalfield House, Arbroath 1948–54

RSA RSW RWA

Black Wall, St Monance, 1958
[ILLUSTRATED]
Oil on board, 55.2 × 75.6
Purchased 1959 with the Morris Trust Fund
23–1959

Window on the Sea, 1965/7
Oil on board, 73.6 × 100.3
Purchased 1968 from the artist with
50% NFA grant
12–1968

Plus two works on paper

Fleming was born in Glasgow and studied lithography, colour woodcut and engraving at Glasgow School of Art. On graduating in 1929 he received a travelling scholarship which allowed him to spend almost two years in England, France and Spain. On his return he qualified as a teacher and turned down a scholarship to the Royal College of Art in London as it would have meant a further three years spent studying. Instead, he completed his important line-engraving *Gethsemane*, which was later purchased by the French government.

In 1931 Fleming joined the staff of Glasgow School of Art, where he was particularly supportive of the students Robert Colquhoun and Robert MacBryde, whom he painted in a celebrated double portrait of 1937–8 (GSA Collection, NMC 020). Fleming served as a reserve policeman as well as in the Pioneer Corps during the Second World War. A fire in 1941 destroyed much of his work. In 1948 Fleming became warden of Hospitalfield House, where he remained until being appointed principal of Gray's School of Art in 1954.

After the war Fleming combined print-making with painting. He visited the picturesque harbour villages along the Scottish north-east coast, from Kirkcaldy to Aberdeen, often with the artist William Wilson (1905–1972). Both men would work outdoors and complete their compositions from memory. Dundee's two paintings by Fleming, *Black Wall, St Monance* and *Window on the Sea* are fine examples of the resultant gentle, perceptive works which were to dominate his artistic output for more than forty years. St Monance, also known as St Monans, is on the Firth of Forth in the East Neuk of Fife, between Elie and Pittenweem. Its architecture reflects the close relationship between the local fishing community and the sea, appearing to grow out of the rocky shores around the harbour. The village was previously called Inverin and Abercrombie but eventually took its name from Saint Monans, who is thought to have lived in a nearby cave.

Fleming retired from Gray's in 1972, ending a long and influential teaching career. In the 1970s he made the mixed-media print series *Creation* and *Comment*, which combined text with semi-abstract compositions exploring the human dilemma. Fleming played a major part in the development of modern Scottish print-making, significantly expanding its significance within the curriculum at Gray's. He was a permanent member of the Council of the Society of Artist-Printmakers and in 1974 was founding chairman of Peacock Printmakers in Aberdeen. He died in the city in 1994.

ALAN FLETCHER

Born Glasgow 1930; died Milan 1958
Studied Glasgow School of Art 1951–7

Young Girl (Girl with Red Hair), *c.*1957
Oil on board, 52.7 × 52.7
Purchased 1968 with 50% NFA grant
4–1968

Still Life with Lamp and Cup (Green, Red and White Still Life), *c.*1957
[ILLUSTRATED]
Oil on board, 46 × 76.2
Purchased 1968 with 50% NFA grant
5–1968

Lamp and Pear, 1957
Oil on board, 83.8 × 57.1
Purchased 1968 with 50% NFA grant
6–1968

Fletcher was born in Glasgow. In 1951, after National Service, he began the general course at Glasgow School of Art. For his diploma he joined the sculpture department under Benno Schotz (1891–1984), graduating in 1957. He became Schotz's assistant and in particular helped him with the commission for the 1958 Altar Cross for St Paul's in Glenrothes. Fletcher was awarded the art school's John Keppie Travelling Scholarship and decided to go to Italy. One night whilst staying in a hostel in Milan he stepped over a parapet, not realising there was a sheer drop on the other side, and died.

Despite his death aged twenty-eight, Fletcher had already begun to exhibit in public, including in Glasgow, Edinburgh, New York and Moscow. Most of his surviving work dates from the last two years of his life, including *Still Life with Lamp and Cup*. In this painting, flat planes of colour and simplified still-life objects are thickly painted on a rough board support, creating a carefully balanced, austere composition and a feeling of rawness and immediacy. This approach suggests that Fletcher was aware of the work of the Russian artist Nicolas de Staël (1914–1955).

Following his death, Schotz organised a memorial exhibition of Fletcher's work, held at the McLellan Galleries, Glasgow, in 1959, which included paintings, drawings and sculpture. In the introduction to the catalogue Schotz declared: 'There is no trace in him of provincialism. His work was in the broad stream of the modern movement, and we, as we look on his paintings now, are left wondering what might not his future have been in terms of paint and invention.'[18] Further exhibitions of Fletcher's work have been held at the Traverse Gallery, Edinburgh, in 1968 and at the North Briton Gallery, Gartocharn, in 1973. William Hardie, Dundee's keeper of art, was so impressed by the 1968 exhibition that he acquired three works from it for the collection.

DAVID FOGGIE

Born Dundee 1878; died Edinburgh 1948

Studied Academy of Fine Arts, Antwerp 1898–1900 and 1902–4

Taught Edinburgh College of Art 1920–39

RSA RSW

Portrait of the Artist's Wife, 1922
[ILLUSTRATED]
Oil on canvas, 91.4 × 71.1
Purchased 1924 with the Morris Trust Fund
22–1924

Forfouchten, 1919
Oil on canvas, 91.4 × 71.1
Presented 1932 by J.C. Low
6–1932

Joseph Lee, 1911
Oil on canvas, 61 × 50.8
Presented 1949 by Mrs Dorothy J. Lee
7–1949

Plus two works on paper

Foggie was born in Dundee and studied in Antwerp's Academy of Fine Arts in 1898–1900 and 1902–4. He spent the intervening and succeeding years based in Tayport and had studios in Dundee at 28 Ward Road and later at 132a Nethergate. Asthma prevented Foggie from serving in the First World War. In 1919 he moved to Edinburgh and the following year began teaching life drawing part-time at Edinburgh College of Art, reflecting his outstanding skills as a draughtsman. Wilhelmina Barns-Graham was amongst his students. He remained on the staff until retirement in 1939.

In his portraiture Foggie avoided an obviously commercial approach and instead preferred to depict manual workers, professional models, friends and members of his own family, particularly his wife Margaret Anne Jack (1878–1975) who can be seen in *Portrait of the Artist's Wife* of 1922. Their son Neil said of this work: 'If my memory serves me correctly when first exhibited it was called 'The Revel Frock' as it was the costume my mother had worn to the Edinburgh College of Art Revels of that year.'[19] It was bought for Dundee Art Gallery in 1924, making it the first painting by Foggie to enter a public collection. He was also a talented etcher, while watercolours of East Lothian and the fishing villages of Fife, made during college holidays, brought him further appreciation.

Foggie was a prominent member of the Scottish art world of the first half of the twentieth century, not just through his association with Edinburgh College of Art. In 1905 he was a founder member of the Tayport Artists' Circle, became president of Dundee Art Society in 1912

and was a member of Aberdeen Artists' Society between 1908 and 1937. In 1918 Foggie was elected to the RSW, becoming vice-president in 1930, the same year in which he was elected to the RSA, serving as secretary from 1932 until his death. He also exhibited with the SSA, RGI, Paisley Art Institute and the Glasgow Society of Painters and Sculptors. Following his death in 1948 memorial exhibitions were held at Edinburgh College of Art and at Doig, Wilson & Wheatley, Edinburgh. Retrospectives have since been mounted at Dundee Art Gallery in 1978 and in the Tower Foyer and Lamb Galleries of the University of Dundee in 2004.

ALEC GRIEVE

Born Dundee 1864; died Dundee 1933
Studied Académie Colarossi, Paris

Miss Agnes Husband, 1910
Oil on canvas, 123.2 × 92.1
Presented 1910 by the sitter
72–1912

Pont du Cheval, Bruges, 1911
[ILLUSTRATED]
Oil on canvas, 51.5 × 61.6
Presented 1912 by William Low
172–1912

Robert Stirton, J.P., 1919
Oil on canvas, 127 × 89.2
Presentation portrait (posthumous), 1919
3–1919

Moonlight Sonata
Oil on canvas, 101.6 × 153.6
Bequeathed 1933 by the artist
3–1933

Sunset on the Tay, 1921
Oil on canvas, 62.2 × 78.7
Presented anonymously by several of the
artist's friends
B.H.1971–49

Pont du Cheval, Bruges, 1922
Oil on canvas, 71.7 × 92.1
Bequeathed 1933 by the artist
B.H.1971–50

Dundee from Tayport, c.1926
Oil on canvas, 63.5 × 78.8
Purchased 1927 with the Morris Trust Fund
B.H.1971–51

The Artist's Wife
Oil on canvas, 88.8 × 66.8
Presented c.1951 by an unknown donor
B.H.1971–52

Lac d'Amour (The Minnewater, Bruges)
Oil on canvas, 48.3 × 58.4
Bequeathed 1933 by the artist
B.H.1971–53

The Moor, Tayport
Oil on canvas, 61 × 76.2
Presented 1987, part of The Orchar Collection
272–1987–363

Street in Tayport
Oil on canvas
Presented 1992 by Mr Webster
2000–62

Newburgh on Tay
Oil on board, 39.4 × 52.1
Presented 1987, part of The Orchar Collection
1999–12–4

Plus two works on paper

Grieve was born in Dundee and studied art at Dundee High School with John Duncan and Stewart Carmichael under William Grubb. He went on to the Académie Colarossi in Paris before working in London with a publishing firm producing etchings and drawings. He returned to Dundee in 1890 to pursue a career as a painter of landscapes.

Pont du Cheval, Bruges of 1911 shows Grieve's subtle use of colour and tonality. It is typical of the work made during his many visits to France and Belgium in the late nineteenth and early twentieth centuries and was probably influenced by the celebrated *Nocturne* series by James McNeill Whistler (1834–1903). The painting was first exhibited, shortly after completion, at the Victoria Art Galleries in 1912 as part of the exhibition *Loan Collection of Paintings, etc., in the Victoria Art Galleries, Dundee on the Occasion of the British Association Meeting.*

Grieve married Emma Willis in 1897 and resided at West Lights, Tayport. As his obituary noted, he found there 'never-ending subject matter, with across the river the great city in all its continually changing aspects.' He found endless inspiration in views of the River Tay, especially at sunset.

Grieve exhibited widely, including at the Royal Academy, London, the Paris Salon and the Royal Scottish Academy, Edinburgh. He was a founder member of the Tayport Artists' Circle in 1905 and also belonged to the Aberdeen Artists' Society and the Society of Scottish Artists. A leading light in the Dundee Graphic Arts Association (later the Dundee Art Society), he played a major role in the artists' community based in Dundee in the 1890s alongside Duncan, George Dutch Davidson and David Foggie. Grieve died in Dundee Royal Infirmary in February 1933 when he was showing twenty-nine oils and sixteen etchings at a three-man show in the Victoria Art Galleries alongside Stewart Carmichael and John Maclauchlan Milne.

JAMES GUNN

Born Glasgow 1893; died London 1964

Studied Glasgow School of Art 1909; Edinburgh
College of Art 1910–11; and Académie Julian, Paris
1911–12

RA RP RSW

William Huntley Buist,
Lord Provost of Dundee 1932–35, 1935
Oil on canvas, 127 × 101.6
Presentation portrait 1935
1971–54

My Wife, c.1933
[ILLUSTRATED]
Oil on canvas, 214 × 116.8
Presented 1938 by the artist
1971–55

Herbert James Gunn was born in Glasgow and
from 1933 signed his works simply 'James Gunn'.
He studied briefly at Glasgow School of Art and
Edinburgh College of Art before moving to Paris
where he enrolled at the Académie Julian. On his
return from France in 1912, Gunn moved to
Edinburgh but also spent time in London where
he was supported by the Bond Street dealer W.B.
Paterson, at whose instigation Gunn spent four
months in Spain in 1914. The following year
Gunn enlisted in the Artists' Rifles and was
commissioned into the 10th Scottish Rifles, 15th
Division, two years later.

After the First World War, Gunn moved to
London and tried to establish himself as an
artist. The year 1929 proved to be a decisive one
for Gunn; the failure to sell his landscapes and
the praise received for his portraiture in a solo
exhibition at The Fine Art Society, London,
encouraged him to devote himself thereafter to
portraiture. In August that year he married
Marie Pauline Miller (1901–1950). Pauline
became his favourite model and his portraits of
her, including *My Wife*, are amongst Gunn's most
celebrated paintings. In contrast to his portraits
of illustrious sitters, including King George VI,
Queen Elizabeth II, the Prime Minister Neville
Chamberlain and Field-Marshall Montgomery,
those he made of his wife show their love and
intimacy and he took obvious pleasure in her
outstanding beauty. In *My Wife*, the elegance of
Pauline's pose matches that of her clothes. The
coat she wears was designed by Elspeth
Champcommunal of Paris and its velvet texture
is meticulously rendered, while the bright
whiteness of her gloves and hairpiece enliven the

deep black of her outfit. Gunn presented the
work to Dundee in 1938, three years after his
portrait of William Huntley Buist, Lord Provost
of Dundee, had entered the city's collection.

Gunn's brilliance of execution and acute
powers of observation meant that he enjoyed a
distinguished post-war career, receiving many
high-profile commissions to paint royalty,
aristocrats, statesmen, dons, bankers and the
like, and he became president of the Royal
Society of Portrait Painters in 1953. However,
despite regularly showing in the Royal Academy's summer exhibitions since 1923 he was not
elected a member until 1961. Gunn also exhibited
regularly at the RSA and RGI, maintaining his
links with Scotland.

Pauline died in 1950. Their daughter Chloë
(b.1930) has stated: 'As far as his work was
concerned, she had been not only the subject
of many of his most memorable pictures but
she had always been allowed to criticise and
comment and he took notice of what she said.
No one else was ever able to do this for him.'[20]
Gunn received a knighthood in the 1963 new
year's honours and died the following year.
A memorial display was included in the Royal
Academy summer exhibition of 1965. A major
exhibition of his work was held at the Scottish
National Portrait Gallery, Edinburgh, in 1994
which toured to The Fine Art Society, London
and Harris Art Gallery, Preston.

JOHN HOUSTON

Born Buckhaven 1930; lives and works Edinburgh

Studied Edinburgh College of Art 1948–53 and Moray
House College of Education, Edinburgh 1954–5

Taught Edinburgh College of Art 1955–89

RSA RGI RSW

Sunset over Moorland, 1973
Oil on canvas, 127 × 152.4
Presented 1976 by the Contemporary Art Society
1–1976

Plus one work on paper

Houston was born in Buckhaven, Fife, and grew up in Windygates on the east coast of Scotland. He studied at Edinburgh College of Art and was awarded a travelling scholarship which allowed him to work in Italy in 1953. On his return to Scotland, Houston trained as a teacher and joined the staff of Edinburgh College of Art in 1955, where he remained until retirement in 1989. Houston married the artist Elizabeth Blackadder (b.1931) in 1956.

The landscape and seascape of his home country has been the dominant subject of Houston's œuvre since he was a student. He often sketches or makes watercolours *en plein air*, which he then works up into oil paintings in his studio, attempting to express the original feeling of his direct personal experience in front of the natural motif.

In 1969 Houston was invited by Mr and Mrs S.C. Johnson of Johnson Wax to paint at their country home at Lake Owen, northern Wisconsin. The flatness of the area and the stimulus provided by an exhibition of modern American painting seen in New York on his return journey, inspired a new direction in Houston's work as shown in *Sunset over Moorland*. Houston has commented about this painting:

In 1972 my wife, Elizabeth Blackadder, and I stayed at Lybster in Caithness where I did quite a number of sketches. I produced all the paintings of Caithness back in my studio in Edinburgh. Most were of seas and skies, this is one of the few I did of the flat moorland interior of Caithness. Most of my paintings are done in my studio from drawings, sketches and memories of the subject. Sometimes you see too much when painting on the spot, this can dilute the first strong impression.

Quite a few of my paintings at this time used the format of a low horizon with the major part of the work being sky. This was a compositional device I had started to use in the late 1960s and early 70s, after painting in north Wisconsin, a very flat state, but with wonderful dominating skies. Many of my oils from the mid-1960s to the mid-1970s were fairly thinly painted with one layer of colour scumbled over underlying layers of colours, a technique developed from my watercolours.

This work and others from Caithness led to a series of oils and watercolours I did on two very productive visits to Harris and Lewis in 1974 and 1975.[21]

Houston's first solo exhibition was at the 57 Gallery, Edinburgh, in 1958 and he has worked and exhibited prodigiously ever since. A retrospective exhibition to mark his seventy-fifth birthday was held at the Scottish National Gallery of Modern Art, Edinburgh, in 2005.

JAMES HOWIE

Born Dundee 1931; lives and works Dundee

Studied Duncan of Jordanstone College of Art, Dundee 1950–5 and Liverpool College of Art 1956–7

Taught Duncan of Jordanstone College of Art, Dundee 1962–5

Wait, 1970
Oil on linen, 162.6 × 177.8
Purchased 1970 from the artist with 50% NFA grant
1–1970

Island, 1969
[ILLUSTRATED]
Oil on canvas, 151.5 × 161.3
Scottish Arts Council Bequest 1997
1998–22

Plus one work on paper

James Howie was born in Dundee and studied at both Duncan of Jordanstone and Liverpool colleges of art. In 1970 his work was included in the influential touring exhibition *Seven Painters in Dundee*, organised by the Scottish Arts Council (the other six were Neil Dallas Brown, Dennis Buchan, Peter Collins, Ian Fearn (b.1934), Jack Knox and James Morrison). Howie's work, in common with that of the other artists selected by the exhibition curator, William Hardie, former keeper of art at Dundee Art Gallery, is characterised by a restrained use of colour, a high degree of refinement of handling and finish and an unwillingness to abandon a figurative mode of expression.

As Howie has explained, *Island* and *Wait* 'are part of an extensive series of images inviting contemplation on the nature of time, our waiting in it and the possibility of new beginnings.'[22] The motif of an island, which sometimes is also a mountain, represents something which has survived over an inordinate length of time. It also stands for one's dreams and hopes. Reaching the island is something that man aspires to, as a place of escape, but that is unattainable, almost at the edge of the world. Whilst living in smog-laden London in the late 1950s and looking forward to moving to the Scottish north-east coast and its clear light, Howie also commented: 'Nature is the source of everything I do. The force of Nature. The power of Nature. In Scotland there is more evidence of Nature – openness, purity of light, the continuing presence of sea and sky.'[23]

Howie creates works which contain a sense of eternity and his working process is painstaking. He has explained:

The paintings are never very smooth, but have a texture. There are no thin washes, but rather a considerable body of opaque paint which has been hacked and scraped to reveal underlying forms and colour. Then there are thin glazings and working back into them. But this is only one way of working that I have employed. Different methods and different materials are often used.[24]

Howie has lived and worked in many places, including the Spanish island of Formentera; Kingston, Jamaica, where he was art director of Macmillan's Advertising; and England, where he was a fellow of the University of Sussex. Since 1978 he has been based in Dundee.

GEORGE LESLIE HUNTER

Born Rothesay 1877; died Glasgow 1931

Still Life, *c*.1918
[ILLUSTRATED]
Oil on canvas, 51.1 × 61.3
Purchased 1946
15–1946

The Big Ginger Jar, 1920s
Oil on board, 61 × 52.1
Purchased 1957
40–1957

A Cottage in Fife, 1920s
Oil on canvas, 64.1 × 76.8
Bequeathed 1974 by William G. Shiell
10–1974

Along with Francis Campbell Boileau Cadell, John Duncan Fergusson and Samuel John Peploe, Hunter is one of the four artists known as the Scottish Colourists. He was born in Rothesay and emigrated with his family to California in 1892. Hunter remained in San Francisco when his relatives returned to Scotland in 1900. A natural draughtsman, much of his early career was spent trying to make a living by providing illustrations for magazines, such as *The Overland Monthly* of San Francisco and the Glaswegian *Society Pictorial*. Due to his time in America, unlike the other Colourists, Hunter did not grow up amidst the flourishing art scenes in Edinburgh and Glasgow of the late nineteenth century. Instead he became part of a Californian circle which included the portrait-sculptor Robert Aitken (1878–1949) and the writer Jack London (1876–1916). He exhibited with the California Society of Artists and the San Francisco Artists' Society and Arts Association.

Like Fergusson, Hunter was self-taught. It is reasonably certain that by 1905 Hunter had visited Paris for an extended period and he continued to make regular visits to France thereafter. In 1906 the work he had prepared for what was to be his first solo exhibition, at the Mark Hopkins Institute in San Francisco, was destroyed by the infamous April earthquake. As a result Hunter returned to live with his mother in Glasgow. Hunter then spent time in London and Paris and had his first solo exhibition in 1913, at Alexander Reid's gallery La Société des Beaux-Arts in Glasgow.

From 1916 until the end of the war Hunter worked on his uncle's farm at Millburn, near Larkhall. He painted Dundee's *Still Life* around 1918. It reveals Hunter's interest in Dutch seventeenth-century painting; its subject matter is directly related to the Dutch tradition, including peeled fruits, flowers, Chinese porcelain and glassware, arranged on a draped table set against a dark background. The luscious painting of the flowers also recalls the work of Edouard Manet (1832–1883). *Still Life* cannot be described as avant garde but it does reveal a skilful manipulation of colour and of oil paint.

Like Cadell, Hunter established his reputation during the 1920s, despite periods of serious ill-health and an unevenness in his work. He worked in Paris, Venice, Florence and Fife, and in 1924 visited California and New York. In 1926 or 1927 Hunter moved to the south of France but ill-health forced him to return to Glasgow in 1929. The following two years he painted at Loch Lomond, having worked there in 1924. His vibrant Loch Lomond paintings are amongst his most celebrated works. He died in Glasgow in 1931 and Reid organised a memorial exhibition shortly afterwards. Hunter was the most independent of the four Scottish Colourists, with whom he has posthumously become more closely associated than he was whilst alive.

WILLIAM JOHNSTONE

Born Denholm, Roxburghshire 1897; died Crailing, Roxburghshire 1981

Studied Edinburgh College of Art 1919–23 and Royal Scottish Academy School of Painting, Edinburgh 1923–5

Taught Camberwell School of Arts and Crafts, London 1938–47 and Central School of Arts and Crafts, London 1947–60

Ode to the North Wind, *c*.1929–31
[ILLUSTRATED]
Oil on canvas, 71.1 × 91.4
Purchased 1971 from the artist with 50% NFA grant
3–1971

Northern Gothic, *c*.1960
Acrylic on canvas, 136.8 × 243.2
Presented 1977 by Mrs Hope Montagu Douglas Scott, Edinburgh
4–1977

Plus one work on paper

Johnstone was born in Denholm in the Scottish Borders and enrolled at Edinburgh College of Art in 1919. He also studied at the Royal Scottish Academy School of Painting, and in 1925 was awarded a travelling scholarship which allowed him to spend two years in Paris, Spain, Italy and North Africa. Johnstone sailed to America in 1928 with his wife, the sculptor Flora MacDonald, and they lived in Carmel, California, until the following August. As a result, Johnstone became interested in Native American Indian sand paintings and rugs, as well as the work of contemporary American artists including Arthur Dove (1880–1946) and Georgia O'Keeffe (1887–1986). After a brief spell in Selkirk the couple moved to London in 1930, where Johnstone was to have a long and distinguished teaching career.

Ode to the North Wind is one of Johnstone's most important paintings. It is an extremely progressive, almost abstract painting and marks Johnstone out, along with William McCance, as one of the most advanced Scottish painters of the inter-war years. It reveals Johnstone's awareness of contemporary developments in art, with which he became familiar at first hand in Paris, combined with research into his national heritage, including Celtic and Pictish art, as he strove to create a new and uniquely Scottish art.

Ode to the North Wind is closely related to Johnstone's other celebrated metamorphic landscapes of the late 1920s and early 1930s, namely *The Garden of the Hesperides*, *c*.1929 and his masterpiece *A Point in Time*, *c*.1929–37 (Scottish National Gallery of Modern Art,

Edinburgh, GMA 1254). As Johnstone explained:

These pictures were motivated from an inner being, the subconscious, and had no relation to the visual world as seen by the photographic eye. In these paintings, too, I was trying to bring back form into painting … [Ode to the North Wind] formed a most important contributing factor in my development.[25]

It has also been argued that the work explores Johnstone's understanding of man's ancient relationship with landscape and of landscape as the site of collective memory and therefore as a source of identity.

Johnstone was appointed principal of Camberwell School of Arts and Crafts in 1938, where he remained until he became principal of the Central School of Arts and Crafts in 1947. He exerted a huge influence on post-war art education in England. Amongst the young artists he appointed as teachers were Alan Davie (b.1920), Kenneth Martin (1905–1984), William Turnbull (b.1922) and Eduardo Paolozzi (1924–2005).

In 1960 Johnstone left the Central School and returned to the Scottish Borders. His work underwent a period of extraordinary renaissance in the last twenty or so years of his life, beginning with the *Northern Gothic Series* of 1958–60 (of which Dundee owns an example) and as seen in the *Genesis* series of plaster reliefs of 1972–3. The 1970 Scottish Arts Council touring retrospective exhibition of his work was the first held in Scotland since 1935. Johnstone died in 1981, the year a major exhibition of his work organised by the Arts Council of Great Britain toured the UK.

HARRY KEAY

Born Dundee 1914; died Kingston on Spey 1994

Studied Dundee College of Art 1935–9, and
Hospitalfield House, Arbroath, summer 1939

Taught Trade School, Dundee c.1945–50 and Morgan
Academy, Dundee 1950–74

Still Life with Lustre Jug, 1941
[ILLUSTRATED]
Oil on canvas, 64 × 76.5
Purchased 1991 with 50% NFA grant and 25% The Art
Fund grant (William Leng Fund)
7–1992

Tulips in a Lustre Jug, 1947
Oil on canvas, 50.8 × 61
Purchased 1950
2–1950

Harry Keay studied at Dundee College of Art, where his work was assessed by Dame Laura Knight. He was awarded a grant to travel in Europe but it is not known if he took advantage of this. He spent the summer of 1939 at Hospitalfield House, Arbroath, where he came under the influence of James Cowie.

Keay was exempt from military service during the war because of a withered right arm but joined the Observer Corps. From 1945 until his retirement in the mid-1970s, Keay devoted his life to teaching art, initially at Dundee's Trade School and then for the majority of his career at Morgan Academy, Dundee, where he became principal teacher of art.

Still Life with Lustre Jug, 1941, may be Keay's masterpiece. He gifted it to Dr Margaret Herring, a well-known Dundee obstetrician. The painting is unusually crisp and hard-edged, revealing the artist's technical excellence. It shows Cowie's influence and also that of his friend and mentor, James McIntosh Patrick. While Keay had an impressive local reputation and is remembered with respect and admiration by many of his pupils at the Morgan Academy, there are no traceable catalogues or reviews of his work. All that appears to have survived is a family album of colour photographs of twenty-three of his paintings, from which it is clear that the intensity and hyper-realism evident in *Still Life with Lustre Jug* is characteristic of Keay's œuvre.

Never a man for solo exhibitions, Keay was best known in the 1940s and 1950s. He exhibited regularly at the RA, the RSA and at the spring and autumn shows of the Dundee Art Society. He moved north after his retirement and died at Kingston on Spey, near Elgin, in 1994.

JACK KNOX

Born Kirkintilloch 1936; lives and works Broughty Ferry

Studied Glasgow School of Art 1953–8; Atelier André Lhote, Paris 1958–9; and American Center, Paris 1959

Taught Duncan of Jordanstone College of Art, Dundee 1965–81 and Glasgow School of Art 1981–92

RSA RSW RGI HFRIAS

Battle of San Romano II, 1968
[ILLUSTRATED]
PVA on canvas, 80.6 × 81.9
Purchased 1968
3–1968

Cafetière and Bread Basket, 1979
Oil on canvas, 64 × 76.5
Purchased 1979 with 50% NFA grant
128–1979

Jack Knox (known professionally as John until the 1970s) was born in Kirkintilloch and studied at Glasgow School of Art. A travelling scholarship enabled him to study in Paris before he taught at Duncan of Jordanstone and Glasgow School of Art.

Battle of San Romano II comes from a celebrated series of works inspired by the tri-partite Renaissance masterpiece of around 1438–40 by the Italian artist Paolo Uccello (*c.*1397–1475). The National Gallery, London, the Musée du Louvre, Paris, and the Galleria degli Uffizi, Florence, each owns one of the three panels, which depict incidents from the 1432 battle between Florence and Siena. Knox recalled seeing the Florence panel:

> *When I saw the 'Rout of San Romano' in Florence many years ago, I was struck by the fact that despite all the frantic activity depicted there was a curious static quality about it. At the same time however the eye was leaping about all over the place from lances to the horses' accoutrements swinging across the surface.*[26]

When he later saw the London panel, he had the opposite reaction, explaining:

> *Being so close to this one, and its being newly cleaned, with the colours so brilliant, the whole thing was an eye-opener. Suddenly it became so active that I felt my eyes belting all over it, so much so that I began to get quite dizzy just keeping up with it all … For me it was like discovering something for the very first time; that far from being static, this painting of Uccello's was a tremendously active thing.*[27]

Knox has further commented: 'There is a contradiction here, but that is what art is about.'[28]

As a result, Knox began to organise visual elements on the surface of a white ground in a manner inspired by his memory of this experience. The San Romano works are almost all square in format and were made on a large scale. They are filled with a vocabulary of enigmatic symbols, some of which were inspired by objects collected on the beach near Knox's home at Carnoustie, such as fishing tackle. These motifs reveal Knox's highly tuned draughtsman's skills and are orchestrated within an ambiguous spatial context over the image surface.

Following his first solo exhibition, held at 57 Gallery in Edinburgh in 1961, Knox has had regular solo shows and has been included in group exhibitions around the world. A major solo exhibition was organised by the Scottish Arts Council and toured around Scotland in 1983–4 and a retrospective of his drawings was held jointly at the Compass Gallery and Cyril Gerber Fine Art in Glasgow in 1998.

ROBERT MACBRYDE

Born Maybole 1913; died Dublin 1966
Studied Glasgow School of Art 1933–8, and
Hospitalfield House, Arbroath, summer 1938

Still Life, 1959
Oil on canvas, 63.8 × 76.5
Presented 1962 by the Contemporary Art Society
10–1962

MacBryde was born in Maybole, Ayrshire, and worked in a local shoe factory for five years before studying at Glasgow School of Art where he met Robert Colquhoun, with whom he lived and worked until the latter's death. His skills as a draughtsman were encouraged by his art school teachers Ian Fleming and Hugh Adam Crawford, as well as by James Cowie, warden of Hospitalfield House where 'the two Roberts', as they were known, spent the summer of 1938. They travelled in France and Italy during 1939 but returned to Ayrshire when war was declared. Colquhoun was enlisted into the Royal Medical Army Corps in 1940, while MacBryde was exempted from service on medical grounds.

On Colquhoun's discharge in 1941 due to ill-health, the Roberts moved to London where they shared a studio with John Minton (1917–1957) and soon found themselves at the centre of artistic life in the capital. The arrival of their cosmopolitan friend the Polish artist Jankel Adler (1895–1949) in 1943 influenced the work of both the younger painters who increasingly looked to Pablo Picasso (1881–1973) and Wyndham Lewis (1882–1957) for inspiration. As a result MacBryde's work became more decorative, his forms flatter and his palette lighter.

Both of the Roberts had solo exhibitions at the Lefevre Gallery, London, in 1943 – Colquhoun's only such show during his life-time. Thus began a period of success and acclaim. MacBryde evolved his characteristic style, mainly expressed through still-life or figurative subjects, in which simplified, interdependent and brilliantly coloured elements, often enclosed in thick black lines, are combined to create a harmonious whole, as seen in *Still Life* of 1959. This painting is infused with spatial ambiguity, as the fruit is presented on a tipped-up table top within a room in which the wall and floor appear to be on the same plane. The cutting open of the fruit exposes their luscious insides, heightened by the bold colouring of the whole image. The window on the right admits light from that side but the resultant shadows of the lemon and fruit bowl do not fall in the same direction, heightening a sense of artificiality. The stylised wood panelling of the wall and pattern of the flooring recall Cubist collage still lifes by Picasso and Georges Braque (1882–1963).

The Roberts worked on lithographs which were printed at Miller's Press in Lewes where they lived from 1947 until 1948 and on costumes and set designs for Léonide Massine's ballet *Donald of the Burthens* which premiered in 1951. That year MacBryde was commissioned to design murals for the passenger liner *SS Oronsay*. Excessive drinking, lack of food and general penury led to a decline in health and productivity of both artists. MacBryde produced fewer works and enjoyed less success than Colquhoun. He was inconsolable following Colquhoun's death in 1962 and died in a road accident in Dublin in 1966. A joint retrospective of the Roberts' work was held at Glasgow Print Studio in 1990.

WILLIAM McCANCE

Born Cambuslang 1894; died Girvan 1970

Studied Glasgow School of Art 1911–15 and Kennedy Street School, Glasgow 1915–16

Controller, Gregynog Press, Newtown 1930–3

Taught Reading University 1944–59

Mediterranean Hill Town, 1923
[ILLUSTRATED]
Oil on canvas, 92.1 × 61
Purchased 1974 from the artist's widow,
Dr Margaret McCance, with 50% NFA grant
7–1974

Seated Figure (Lucy), 1929
Oil on canvas, 35.6 × 26.4
Presented 1977 by Dr Margaret McCance
3–1977

Plus one work on paper and one sculpture

McCance was born in Cambuslang and studied at Glasgow School of Art. On graduating he trained to be a teacher. During the war he was imprisoned as a conscientious objector but was given leave to marry fellow art student Agnes Miller Parker (1895–1980) in 1918. Following his discharge in 1920 the couple moved to London.

McCance's paintings of the 1920s, including *Mediterranean Hill Town*, occupy a unique place in Scottish art. With the exception of William Johnstone, no other Scottish painter responded with such originality to the avant-garde developments centred on Paris in the early twentieth century. In London, McCance became part of a group which included artists such as Eric Kennington (1888–1960) and the Vorticists William Roberts (1895–1980) and Wyndham Lewis (1882–1957), who shared his interest in pre-war Cubism. By 1922 McCance had developed a highly stylised approach to painting, with a dynamic sense of three-dimensional form. As Patrick Elliott has written,

> Mediterranean Hill Town *of 1923 is undoubtedly one of McCance's most successful landscape paintings and was begun after visiting the small town of Bogliasco in Italy, its viaduct visible in the distance. The curved and cubic structures are fitted together with great mastery, making the hillside seem almost like a living, breathing organism, bursting with energy.*[29]

Shortly after painting *Mediterranean Hill Town*, McCance made a linocut based on its composition.

However, at the time McCance's role as a critic brought him more recognition than his painting, and he was art critic at *The Spectator* from 1923 until 1926. He also contributed cartoons and illustrations to publications including *Lloyds Magazine* and *The Free Man*, edited by Hugh MacDiarmid (1892–1978). MacDiarmid was leader of the Scottish Renaissance, which aimed to encourage a specifically Scottish culture and of which McCance became an enthusiastic supporter.

In addition to painting, McCance was an outstanding printmaker. This informed his work as controller of the renowned Gregynog Press in Newtown, Montgomeryshire (now Powys) from 1930 until 1933. The finely crafted, limited edition books produced during his time there are considered amongst the best ever produced by British private presses. In 1933 the couple moved to a windmill in Albrighton, near Wolverhampton and then to Hambledon, near Henley on Thames, and McCance's interest returned to writing, in particular about economic theory. He was appointed lecturer in typography and book production at the School of Art at Reading University in 1944, where he remained until his retirement in 1959. He separated from Miller Parker in 1955 and in 1963 married Dr Margaret Chislett (b.1926). In that year they settled in Girvan.

McCance exhibited infrequently during his lifetime. His first solo exhibition was held at Reading Museum and Art Gallery in 1960. McCance died in 1970. The variety of his interests and professional positions meant that he never secured the reputation of avant-garde painter that his works of the 1920s would merit, but posthumous exhibitions, in particular those held at the Richard Demarco Gallery, Edinburgh, in 1971, at Dundee Art Gallery in 1975 (which subsequently toured Glasgow and Edinburgh), and at the Scottish National Gallery of Modern Art, Edinburgh, in 1990 have since helped to secure his standing.

DAVID McCLURE

Born Lochwinnoch 1926; died Dundee 1998

Studied Glasgow University 1943–4; Edinburgh University and Edinburgh College of Art 1947–9; and Edinburgh College of Art 1949–52

Taught Edinburgh College of Art 1953–5 and Duncan of Jordanstone College of Art, Dundee 1957–85

RSA RSW

The Ritualists, 1962
[ILLUSTRATED]
Oil on board, 88 × 124
Purchased 1963 with the Morris Trust Fund
4–1963

Girl in an Orange Studio, 1969/77
Oil on canvas, 101.6 × 127
Purchased 1982 from the artist with 50% NFA grant
13–1982

Flowers in Vase and Chalice, 1994
Oil and pastel on canvas laid on board, 76.8 × 63.5
Bequeathed 2003 by Mrs Diana Maud Stirling King through The Art Fund
2004–126

Plus two works on paper

McClure was born in Lochwinnoch, Renfrewshire, in 1926. War service as a 'Bevin Boy' cut short his English studies at Glasgow University. After the war he undertook the joint Fine Art Degree course at Edinburgh University and Edinburgh College of Art. In 1949 he switched to the full-time Drawing and Painting diploma course at the art college. He was elected to the SSA in 1951, a year before graduating. A travelling scholarship allowed him to work in Spain from 1952 until 1953. On his return to Britain, an Andrew Grant Fellowship from Edinburgh College of Art resulted in McClure teaching part-time at the college for two years and working in Florence and Sicily. In 1957 he joined the staff of Duncan of Jordanstone, eventually succeeding Alberto Morrocco as head of painting in 1982. He served as president of the SSA between 1967 and 1969.

McClure's work sits firmly within the tradition of twentieth-century Scottish painting, characterised by strength of colour and confident handling of paint. He was one of a group of highly regarded young painters, including John Houston, Elizabeth Blackadder (b.1931) and David Michie (b.1928), who graduated from Edinburgh College of Art in the early 1950s. Of the density of artistic talent at the college and in the capital at the time, McClure's early work was perhaps most influenced by his tutor John Maxwell (1905–1962), whilst he was also in sympathy with senior figures of the Edinburgh School such as Robert Henderson Blyth (1919–1970), William Gillies (1898–1973), Anne Redpath and William MacTaggart (1903–1981).

The Ritualists is an early work from an important series based on McClure's experience living and working in Florence and Sicily during 1956 to 1957, as well as his previous work made in Spain. In the painting he explored the ceremony, symbolism and colour at the heart of much Catholic worship. He painted a second version of the subject with the same title a year later (property of the artist's family), which includes a seated male nude. After three months painting in Norway in 1963, McClure was once more inspired by memories of Sicily. He painted several further works in which earlier, relatively benign religious subjects became ever more sinister, in biting satirical commentaries on the power and influence of both the Church and organised crime in Italy.

Perhaps more typical of the warmth and optimism which characterised much of McClure's œuvre are two other paintings in Dundee's collection: *Girl in an Orange Studio*, reveals his interest in the Post-Impressionist masters, particularly Matisse, whilst the theme of a model in a studio appeared in his work from time to time over a long period. *Flowers in Vase and Chalice* celebrates the abundance and fecundity of nature in a sumptuous display of blooms. In his maturity, McClure pushed his use of colour towards further brilliance and drama before his death at home in Dundee in 1998.

TALBERT McLEAN

Born Dundee 1906; died Dundee 1992

Studied Dundee College of Art 1923–7 and Dundee College of Education 1927–8

Taught Dundee College of Art 1928–32; Webster's Seminary, Kirriemuir 1946–8; Arbroath High School 1948–62; and Arbroath Academy 1962–72

Reflection, *c.*1952–8
Oil on board, 69.8 × 88.2
Purchased 1959
2–1959

McLean was born in Dundee and studied design at Dundee College of Art. He trained as an art teacher at the city's College of Education and afterwards taught part-time at the art college. From 1933 until 1937 he lived in London where he established himself as a successful cartoonist. Following the death of his parents in 1937, McLean moved to Liverpool and in 1938 married Dorothy Gladhill (b.1916), before living in Tafern-y-Gelyn in north Wales and then in Kirriemuir in Angus. During the war he served with the Royal Tank Regiment of the 10th Battalion. He was transferred to the Royal Engineers and posted to the ordnance section, at Ruabon, north Wales where he became friends with the artist William Scott, before serving in North Africa. McLean returned to Kirriemuir on being demobbed in 1946. He began a long career teaching in Angus schools, through which he came to know James Cowie.

Reflection reveals McLean's considered exploration of abstraction. Its formality and disciplined handling reveal his sympathy with the art of painters such as Scott, Cowie, Edward Bawden (1903–1989) and the English artist Ben Nicholson (1894–1982). The flat planes of colour contrast with the implied volume of the reflected lemon and the booklet behind it. It is work characterised by order and serenity. The painting is difficult to date any more precisely than 1952–8.

As his son, the artist John McLean (b.1939), has explained:

> The Melon, *c.1958* [University of Edinburgh Collection, EU 239] *is set up similarly to* Still life with Lamp and Eggs, *1958* [Private Collection, Scotland] *and together with* Reflection, *forms a group of three works in which my father was making his way gradually towards a more absolute abstraction. This he eventually arrived at when he completed* Perilous Yellow [Private Collection, Scotland] *in 1964. No one in Scotland before him had made a more abstract painting than that.*[30]

McLean became a member of the SSA in 1963 and throughout the 1960s showed at the RGI and the RSA. He retired from teaching in 1972 and as a result was able to dedicate himself to painting. His first solo exhibition was held at the Talbot Rice Gallery in Edinburgh the following year. McLean's later work was handled more freely, partly inspired by his son and by American painters such as Morris Louis (1912–1962) and Mark Rothko (1903–1970), whose work he saw exhibited in London. Throughout his career McLean maintained an independent approach to his work and enjoyed little recognition. He died in Dundee in 1992. As his son has written: 'For my father, abstraction was not severed from the world we see. It was a distillation of reality.'[31]

WILL MACLEAN

Born Inverness 1941; lives and works Tayport and Dundee

Studied Gray's School of Art, Aberdeen 1961–5; Hospitalfield House, Arbroath, summer 1965; and Dundee College of Education 1969–70

Taught Bell Baxter High School, Cupar 1971–81 and Duncan of Jordanstone College of Art and Design, Dundee 1981 to date

RSA RSW RGI

Requiem Construction (John Maclean), 1974
[ILLUSTRATED]
Box construction with found and painted objects, 34.6 × 26 × 9
Purchased 1979 from the artist with the Morris Trust Fund
126–1979

Northern Totem, 1975
Box construction with wood, metal, slate and dogfish skin, 50.7 × 56 × 10
Presented 1979 by the Contemporary Art Society
132–1979

Skye Fisherman – In Memoriam, 1989
Painted relief incorporating found objects, 129.5 × 119.4 × 9
Purchased 1989 with 50% NFA grant
15–1989

The Forefather's Tale, 1974
Box construction with mixed media, 46 × 39 × 9
Scottish Arts Council Bequest 1997
1998–28

Plus twelve works on paper

Maclean was born in Inverness and spent his childhood there and on Skye. He completed a course at HMS Conway before joining the merchant navy. His career as a sailor ended when he failed a sight test, although he has since spent time working as a fisherman. Maclean returned to Scotland in 1959, attended evening classes at Edinburgh College of Art and later studied at Gray's School of Art. A travelling scholarship allowed him to work in Greece, Italy and France.

Requiem Construction (John Maclean) is one of the first of the box constructions which are central to Maclean's œuvre. He made it in 1974, a year after beginning his epic project, *The Ring Net* (Scottish National Gallery of Modern Art, Edinburgh, GMA 2130), a conceptual, documentary exhibition about inshore fishing off the Scottish west coast. *Requiem Construction* continued the model-making involved in *The Ring Net*. The found and made objects it contains could be carried around in his pocket and worked on from time to time as his then teaching responsibilities allowed.

Maclean has recalled:
This work was one of the first box constructions / small sculptures that I made in the 1970s. It was a work in memory of my father Captain John Maclean (1896–1963), Harbour Master, Inverness. The image includes a pilot Captain's cap badge and a number of found and painted objects including oak apples and the image of the fish is cast in lead. My work during this time often included found and painted objects. Later works used moulds and casts from made and found objects with more textured and drawn surfaces.[32]
The objects in this work, as in many of Maclean's box constructions, encapsulate personal memories and historical associations not only from the artist's life but also from the traditional culture of Scottish fisherfolk. Duncan Macmillan has suggested that the implication of a church window relates to Maclean's experiences of the Kirk, that the oak apples attached to twigs have druidic associations, as well as representing the light on the model ship which John Maclean used to teach navigation, and that the abacus beads recall the mathematics which underlie the science as well as attending primary school.[33] The combination of techniques with which the objects are made, from painted to casting to direct assemblage of ready-mades like the cap badge, recall traditional marine carvings and hand-made tools as well as flotsam and jetsam.

Maclean's first solo exhibition was at the British School in Rome in 1967 and he has exhibited regularly since. A retrospective of his constructions and drawings was held at Kirkcaldy Museum and Art Gallery in 1984 *The Ring Net* has been shown extensively throughout Scotland, including at the Scottish National Gallery of Modern Art, Edinburgh, in 1987; a retrospective exhibition toured Scotland in 1992 and the *Driftworks* exhibition was shown at Dundee Contemporary Arts in 2001 followed by Orkney, London and New York. Maclean is currently professor of visual arts and senior research fellow at Duncan of Jordanstone.

JOHN MACLAUCHLAN MILNE

Born Buckhaven 1885; died Greenock 1957
RSA

A Fife Landscape, 1920
Oil on canvas, 101.6 × 127
Purchased 1924 with the Morris Trust Fund
16–1924

Glenelg, 1936
Oil on canvas, 101.6 × 127
Purchased 1936 with the Ower Bequest Fund
5–1936

The Sound of Sleat, 1934
Oil on canvas, 50.8 × 61
Presented 1944 by the heirs of the late
George L. Harvey
5–1944

Seascape, 1920
Oil on canvas, 34.3 × 44.4
Provenance Unknown
B.H.1971–90

Loch Tulla, *c.*1930
Oil on canvas, 100.3 × 125.7
Presented 1987, part of The Orchar Collection
272–1987–228

Larig Ghru, *c.*1930
[ILLUSTRATED]
Oil on canvas, 86.4 × 113.7
Presented 1987, part of The Orchar Collection
272–1987–229

St Tropez, 1953
Oil on canvas, 55.5 × 38.4
Bequeathed 1988 by Mr and Mrs G.D. Robinson
through The Art Fund
10–1988

Plus two works on paper

Maclauchlan Milne was born in Buckhaven and grew up in Edinburgh. His father was the painter Joseph Milne (1861–1911) and he was named after John Maclauchlan, chief librarian and curator of Dundee Art Gallery and Museum. In the mid-1900s Maclauchlan Milne emigrated to Canada and spent several years working as a cowboy before returning via Paris to Scotland to paint, mainly in Fife.

During the First World War Maclauchlan Milne served in the Royal Flying Corps. Between 1919 and 1932 he spent significant parts of each year in France, initially in Paris and then in the Midi, particularly in St Tropez. Like his friend Samuel John Peploe, Maclauchlan Milne was greatly inspired by the French Post-Impressionst painter Paul Cézanne (1839–1906) and this, combined with his experience of France, brought about a dramatic change in his work after the war. His early atmospheric paintings, which showed an interest in seventeenth-century Dutch painting, gave way to brightly coloured, boldly painted French landscape scenes. These earn him the right to be called a 'Scottish Colourist' and indeed he painted alongside Peploe and F. C. B. Cadell in France and described George Leslie Hunter as a good friend.

From 1922 Maclauchlan Milne had a studio at 132a Nethergate in the centre of Dundee and built up a loyal, local clientele including Alexander Keiller, head of the renowned Dundee marmalade manufacturing firm, who sponsored his painting trips to France, and the local businessman Fred Lawson. However, the worsening economic situation in Europe curtailed Maclauchlan Milne's extended visits to France. Instead he applied his vision to painting landscapes of the west Highlands, which constitute the bulk of the work of his maturity. He would often explore the area with Lawson in the latter's motor caravan, converted from a First World War ambulance.

Larig Ghru of around 1930, is a good example of the work which resulted from such trips. The palette of the sky, tinged with the greys of implied bad weather and the monumentality of the snow-covered mountains, recall Cézanne, while the softer, more fertile foreground with delicately rendered trees relate to Maclauchlan Milne's depiction of the dry landscape of the south of France. The Lairig Ghru is possibly the best known high level pass in Scotland. It cuts north to south through the Cairngorm plateau and provides a spectacular walking route.

The contraction of his Dundee-based market during the 1930s and his love of the west of Scotland saw Maclauchlan Milne move to the island of Arran in 1939. The island landscape and seascape, in particular the area around Sannox and Corrie, became a new source of inspiration for his late work.

Maclauchlan Milne returned to the mainland as a visiting artist at Hospitalfield House from July to September 1956. He died the following year; a memorial display of his work was held at the RSA in 1958. In 1985 Dundee Art Gallery staged a centenary exhibition of the work of this lesser-known Scottish Colourist.

JAMES MORRISON

Born Glasgow 1932; lives and works Montrose

Studied Glasgow School of Art 1950–4

Taught Denniston Junior Secondary School, Glasgow 1955; Wishaw Junior Secondary 1956–8; Mackie Academy, Stonehaven 1958–65; and Duncan of Jordanstone College of Art, Dundee 1965–87

RSA RSW

Back Court, Rotten Row, Glasgow, 1955
Oil on canvas, 75.6 × 127
Purchased 1959 with the Morris Trust Fund
24–1959

Denhead Farm, 1964
[ILLUSTRATED]
Oil on canvas, 61.6 × 91.4
Purchased 1967 with the Morris Trust Fund
1–1967

The Wood in Winter, 1981
Oil on hardboard, 31 × 53.5
Presented 2000 by Miss Barbara Wishart
2001–30

Plus one work on paper

Morrison was born in Glasgow and studied at the city's School of Art, graduating in 1954. He established his reputation with a celebrated series of paintings of Glasgow's decaying Victorian tenement and terrace architecture, begun in the late 1950s and including Dundee's *Back Court, Rotten Row, Glasgow* of 1955.

Three years later Morrison moved to Catterline, Kincardineshire, where he lived until 1965. The change of environment from the great industrial city of Glasgow to the soft beauty of the fertile, farmed Kincardine countryside was immediately reflected in his work, as can be seen in *Denhead Farm*. This painting veers between abstraction and realism and features agricultural architecture, mainly depicted in black and isolated within its rural setting, perhaps recalling the thickly begrimed buildings surrounded by the remnants of demolition which had concerned the artist before.

Morrison has commented on *Denhead Farm*: *Painted while I lived in Catterline, this is one of a number of works based on a farm on the coast south of Stonehaven. By 1964 I had been painting at that precise location for three years. In the early 1960s I worked in two distinct manners depending on whether the work was painted in the studio or outdoors. This work was painted outside and the colours are derived from the winter landscape. The issues which then interested me revolved around the dynamic relationship between the forms of the organic landscape and the geometric forms of the buildings. These concerns were filtered through a sensibility which was concerned with the abstract relationships of forms and colour. This interest had been given impetus by a 1960 visit to Paris and a close study of the painting of Nicolas de Staël (1914–1955), in particular his ability to invest meaning in sub-rectangular passages of paint, their relationships to each other and to the whole, the entirety in a non-representational but suggestively organic manner. My later work, though a partial rejection of abstraction in a search for a less rootless subjectivity, has prompted a shift in interest from the process of art towards the processes of the world.*[34]

With Alan Fletcher, Morrison helped to found the Glasgow Group in 1958, established to promote the visual arts in the west of Scotland and still in existence today. Since 1965 Morrison has lived in Montrose, where he was art director of the Montrose Festival from 1966 until 1969. He taught at Duncan of Jordanstone for over twenty years and his work has maintained a deep connection with nature. This has most recently and spectacularly been seen in his images of the Canadian High Arctic painted during several trips made throughout the 1990s. He exhibits regularly and successfully with The Scottish Gallery, Edinburgh.

ALBERTO MORROCCO

Born Aberdeen 1917; died Dundee 1998

Studied Gray's School of Art, Aberdeen 1932–8

Taught Gray's School of Art, Aberdeen 1946–9 and
Duncan of Jordanstone College of Art, Dundee 1950–82

RSA RSW RP

The Attic Bedroom, 1955
[ILLUSTRATED]
Oil on canvas, 130.8 × 80
Purchased 1956 with the Morris Trust Fund
2–1956

Still Life on Red Cloth, 1986
[ILLUSTRATED]
Oil on canvas, 101.6 × 117.5
Purchased 1987 with 50% NFA grant
268–1987

Riders on a Beach, 1959
[ILLUSTRATED]
Oil on board, 120.2 × 145.1
Scottish Arts Council Bequest 1997
1998–33

Window in Orbitello, c.1975
Oil on board, 61 × 30.5
Bequeathed 2003 by Mrs Diana Maud Stirling King
through The Art Fund
2004–125

Plus one work on paper

Alberto Morrocco was born in Aberdeen in 1917 to first generation immigrant Italian parents. At the age of fourteen he joined Gray's School of Art, where the fine draughtsmanship of James Cowie and the interest in Italian Renaissance art of Robert Sivell (1888–1958), two of his teachers, had a long-lasting influence on his work. After graduating in 1938, Morrocco was awarded two travelling scholarships which allowed him to work in France and Switzerland before the outbreak of the Second World War. He joined the 51st Highland Division but after Italy entered the war Morrocco was posted to Edinburgh Castle with other Scots of dual nationality, where he remained for three and a half years.

In 1941 Morrocco married Vera Mercer (b.1921) and after the war they moved to Aberdeen, where he worked part-time at Gray's. In 1950 he was appointed head of painting at Duncan of Jordanstone College of Art where he remained until retirement in 1982 and in which position he is credited with the emergence of the college as one of the best art schools in Britain. During the 1950s he produced a series of gentle paintings of domestic scenes, including *The Attic Bedroom*, which features his wife and reflects his pleasure in family life. These intimate, neo-impressionist images reveal an interest in the French artist Edouard Vuillard (1868–1940), whose work Morrocco is likely to have seen in a joint exhibition with Pierre Bonnard (1867–1947) held during the Edinburgh International Festival in 1948.

Morrocco visited Italy for the first time since childhood in 1950 and returned regularly thereafter, in particular to the hill town of Anticoli Corrado. Experiences and images of Italian daily life became one of the most frequently recurring themes of his work. In *Riders on a Beach*, Morrocco depicted one of the most visually thrilling moments of his life. One evening on a beach in Sicily he watched as a group of young men removed their clothes and rode straight into the sea to remove the dirt of a day's work, exuberantly shouting and circling round each other in the water, in an event which to the artist had a primeval quality to it. By this time, Morrocco's brushwork had become much more expressive and his colours more raw than the refined handling and palette of earlier in the decade. His forms are simpler and more solid, revealing a sympathy with the work of Pablo Picasso (1881–1973) and Marino Marini (1901–1980).

Morrocco is widely known for the warmth, sensuality and graphic strength of his paintings, as well as for the bravura combination of vivid colours which came to characterise much of his later work, as can be seen in *Still Life on Red Cloth* of 1986, which is a fine example of this important genre in his œuvre. Part of his art college training was based on the still life, a genre Morrocco continued to paint for the rest of his life, most enthusiastically from the 1970s. In 1993 he explained, 'you can actually use the shapes within a still life just as you would in an abstract because they don't necessarily have to tell any story – apart from their own existence.'[35] Referring to Dundee's painting he commented:

If you are interested in colour, you want to get the full powerful value of it ... So I started to use colour, trying to push it to the absolute limit of

intensity within its range. That painting ...
was one of these – using a variety of reds, with
blue in some and orange in others – but all reds
– red base – acting on each other with both a
harmony and a discord.[36]

Morrocco was greatly in demand as a portrait painter and was the recipient of many prestigious commissions, including one of 1973 to paint Her Majesty The Queen Mother. He began exhibiting regularly at the RSA in 1939 and had the first of over thirty solo shows at the British Council Gallery in Aberdeen in 1949. A major retrospective exhibition of his work was mounted at the McManus Galleries and Museum in 1993, to celebrate his seventy-fifth birthday, which toured to Aberdeen, Edinburgh and Milngavie. He was awarded an OBE in 1993. Morrocco died in Dundee in 1998. He is one of the city's most celebrated artists, due both to his position as head of painting at Duncan of Jordanstone for over thirty years and to his success as one of Scotland's foremost post-war painters.

The Attic Bedroom, 1955

Riders on a Beach, 1959

Still Life on Red Cloth, 1986

JAMES McINTOSH PATRICK

Born Dundee 1907; died Dundee 1998
Studied Glasgow School of Art 1924–8
Taught intermittently Dundee College of Art 1930– 96
RSA ROI ARE

The Right Revd Monsignor Canon Turner, 1932
Oil on canvas, 111.7 × 76.2
Presented 1932 by the sitter
12–1932

A City Garden, 1940
[ILLUSTRATED]
Oil on canvas, 71.1 × 91.4
Purchased 1940 with the Ower Bequest Fund
2–1940

Autumn, Kinnordy, 1936
[ILLUSTRATED]
Oil on canvas, 76.8 × 102.2
Presented 1946 by the Hon. Mrs Charles H. Lyell in
memory of Capt. the Hon. Charles Anthony, Lord
Lyell of Kinnordy VC, and the men of the Scottish
Regiments who fell in the 1939–45 War
25–1946

The Tay Bridge from my Studio Window, 1948
[ILLUSTRATED]
Oil on canvas, 76.2 × 101.6
Purchased 1962
18–1962

The Tay Road Bridge, 1966
Oil on canvas, 63.5 × 76.2
Presented 1968 by Valentine & Sons, Dundee
1–1968

A City Garden, 1979
Acrylic on canvas, 75 × 113.7
Presented 1983 in loving memory of Janet Patrick by
her husband and family

Glen Bran, Abernyte, 1952
Oil on canvas, 62.2 × 74.9
Presented 1987, part of The Orchar Collection
272–1987–367

Easdale, 1928
Oil on board, 33 × 46.5
Presented 1998 by the artist's family through The Fine
Art Society, London
1998–155

At Gairloch, 1929
Oil on board, 27 × 37
Presented 1998 by the artist's family through The Fine
Art Society, London
1998–156

The Weaving Shed, Old Glamis Factory, 1929
Oil on canvas, 44 × 59.5
Purchased 2001 with 50% NFA grant and donation
from The A. Sinclair Henderson Trust
2001–22

Plus twenty-eight works on paper and a range of
archival material including the artist's paints and
brushes

McIntosh Patrick was born in Dundee and is one
of the city's most celebrated artists. He enrolled
at Glasgow School of Art in 1924, starting in the
second year of the course because of the quality
of his portfolio. He graduated in 1927 and
completed a post-diploma year in 1928. He first
found success as an etcher but the market for
etchings collapsed during the Great Depression
prompting him to concentrate on painting.

Autumn, Kinnordy, 1936, is the third in the
artist's celebrated Four Seasons series which
made Patrick's reputation as a landscape painter.
The others are *Winter in Angus*, 1935 in the Tate,
London (N04818), *Springtime in Eskdale*, 1935, in
the Walker Art Gallery, Liverpool (WAG 2597)
and *Midsummer in East Fife*, 1936, in Aberdeen Art
Gallery (ABDAG 003048). The four paintings are
'composite' pictures, based on sketches of
landscape features which were later worked up
in the studio into elaborate, realist compositions. Based on a watercolour made on the spot,
the view in Dundee's painting is from Castle Hill,
Kinnordy. It is an accurate depiction of the
rolling countryside which stretches away to the
northeast towards Laurencekirk.

A City Garden, one of McIntosh Patrick's most
accomplished paintings, was purchased by
Dundee in 1940, the year in which it was made

and exhibited at the RA in London. It shows
the artist's back garden, which he painted
while waiting to be called up to the army. He
explained: 'The war being on made all the little
intimate things suddenly very precious and
there was no knowing but that the Tay Bridge
would be bombed next week.'[37] McIntosh
Patrick's wife, Janet, is depicted hanging out the
washing while his daughter, Ann, is delving into
the clothes basket. On the left, an Anderson air-
raid shelter is being excavated. McIntosh
Patrick painted the same subject in 1979,
showing the results of some forty years of
gardening. This work, of the same title, was
given to Dundee by the artist's family in
memory of Janet.

The Tay Bridge from My Studio Window of 1948
was McIntosh Patrick's first major painting
after the war. It shows the view from the front of
his house, as opposed to from the back, as in the
City Garden works. Magdalen Green, the Tay
estuary and its railway bridge are visible, whilst
the artist painted the railings from memory, as
they had been removed as part of the war effort.
The artist explained: 'I always had the idea of
painting two pictures constituting two views, as
it were, from the same spot. *A City Garden* was
the view to the north of the house and in due
course I painted the Tay Bridge as the view to the
south.'[38] Janet stands at the gate with Lulu, the
dog, while their son Andrew is riding the
bicycle. David MacDonald, a stockbroker and
dog-breeder, walks on the edge of the green with
his pack of dogs. The horse and cart belonged to
Roy, the fruit merchant.

After the war McIntosh Patrick became one

Autumn, Kinnordy, 1936

of Scotland's most successful painters, known for highly detailed, panoramic landscape views. He developed a new realistic approach to landscape painting, aiming for complete naturalism and a feeling of immediacy. He wanted to make the countryside and the weather in his paintings as real for the viewer as it had been for him when he experienced them, whilst working outdoors. He became a familiar figure sketching in the Angus and Perthshire countryside in all weathers.

McIntosh Patrick's personal popularity in Dundee was incredible. His work was known to many thousands through the highly popular colour prints of his paintings. In 1979 he was Dundee's Citizen of the Year. Three major retrospective exhibitions for his sixtieth, eightieth and ninetieth birthdays were held at Dundee Art Gallery, the largest in 1987 being visited by 44,560 people in six weeks. In 1986 he was the first artist to be awarded an Honorary Fellowship of Duncan of Jordanstone College of Art (formerly known as Dundee College of Art). He taught his final Saturday morning class at the college, which had run continuously since the late forties, in June 1996, and died in Dundee in 1998.

A City Garden, 1940

The Tay Bridge from my Studio Window, 1948

SAMUEL JOHN PEPLOE

Born Edinburgh 1871; died Edinburgh 1935

Studied Royal Scottish Academy Life School, Edinburgh 1892–6, Académies Julian and Colarossi, Paris 1894

Taught Edinburgh College of Art 1933–4

RSA

Roses and Fan, c.1930
[ILLUSTRATED]
Oil on canvas, 45.7 × 40.6
Purchased 1944 with the Ower Bequest Fund
12–1944

Mixed Fruit: Melon, Grapes and Apples, c.1926
Oil on canvas, 45.7 × 40.6
Purchased 1956
32–1956

The Black Shawl, c.1904
Oil on canvas, 50.8 × 40.6
Presented 1984 by David Murray Burns in memory of his grandfather D.M. Brown (1864–1934)
12–1984

Peploe is the eldest of the four artists known as the Scottish Colourists. The others are F. C. B. Cadell, John Duncan Fergusson and George Leslie Hunter. Peploe was born in Edinburgh and was briefly apprenticed to the legal firm Scott & Glover. In 1892 he left to pursue painting and studied at the RSA Life School until 1896, except for a period spent in Paris – like the other Colourists, Peploe was drawn to the French capital and studied there around 1894. He returned to paint in France frequently, sometimes working alongside Fergusson, until 1910 when he married Margaret Mackay (1874–1959) and they moved to Paris. Through Fergusson, Peploe became acquainted with the Parisian avant garde and the latest developments in French painting, although he was never as intimately involved with them as his friend. In Paris, Peploe's earlier interest in the work of nineteenth-century French painters, particularly Edouard Manet (1832–1883) and seventeenth-century Dutch painters, particularly Frans Hals (1580–1666) gave way to a more contemporary and expressive approach, using rich colours applied with more structured brushstrokes.

In 1912 Peploe returned to Edinburgh and slowly began to build a successful career as an exhibiting artist. His application to join the army after the outbreak of the First World War was rejected on health grounds. From 1918 until 1932 Peploe worked in a studio at 54 Shandwick Place, where he painted *Roses and Fan*. From around 1914 until his death, Peploe sought to paint the perfect still life. A modest selection of props, including roses or tulips, fans, books, fruits and Chinese vases were carefully placed in infinite varieties on patterned drapery. In 1929 he explained: 'There is so much in mere objects, flowers, leaves, jugs, what not – colours, forms, relation – I can never see mystery coming to an end.'[39] In *Roses and Fan* a complicated composition leads the eye from the apple in the foreground to the roses and down to the shallow blue bowl. The unrefined, broad brushstokes mean that elements such as the fan and the drapery are suggested but not defined.

The care which Peploe lavished on his still lifes, painted in the studio, contrasts with the more spontaneous technique with which he created his French and Scottish landscapes, painted *en plein air* from 1896. In 1920, Cadell invited him to paint beside him on Iona and Peploe returned almost annually over the next thirteen years, also working in other parts of Scotland and France. In 1927 Peploe was the first of the Colourists to receive official recognition from the Scottish establishment when he was elected to the RSA. Following his death in 1935, memorial exhibitions were held at Aitken Dott & Son, Edinburgh, in 1936 and at the McLellan Galleries, Glasgow, in 1937. Significant posthumous solo exhibitions have included those at the National Gallery of Scotland, Edinburgh, in 1941, an Arts Council Scottish Committee touring exhibition of 1953 and a commemorative exhibition at the Scottish National Gallery of Modern Art, Edinburgh, in 1985.

ROBIN PHILIPSON

Born Broughton-in-Furness, Cumbria 1916; died
Edinburgh 1992

Studied Edinburgh College of Art 1936–40 and Moray
House College of Education, Edinburgh 1946–7

Taught Edinburgh College of Art 1947–82

RSA RSW RA

Crucifixion, 1966/80
Oil, tempera and gesso on canvas, 137.2 × 91.4
Purchased 1980 with 50% NFA grant
14–1980

Plus one work on paper

Philipson was born in Cumbria in 1916 and moved to Gretna in 1930. He studied at Edinburgh College of Art. Shortly after graduating he was conscripted into the King's Own Scottish Borderers and served in India, Burma and Singapore. He joined the staff of Edinburgh College of Art in 1947, remaining until retirement in 1982. With William Gillies (1898–1973), John Maxwell (1905–1962), William MacTaggart (1903–1981) and Anne Redpath, Philipson was amongst the most prominent and expressionist members of the so-called Edinburgh School.

Philipson originally made *Crucifixion* in 1966 and worked on it again in 1980. He often pursued themes over a number of years, sometimes developing several in tandem. This painting comes from a series on the subject of Christ's death made in the late 1960s. They relate to earlier images of the interiors of French cathedrals, in particular their rose windows, and of Mexican altars. The crucifixion works are also associated with an angst-ridden series inspired by the First World War. Thus, in this painting Philipson's interest in the framework provided by a religious architectural context and the rich colour created by light shining through stained glass (and splitting into the rainbow spectrum as shown at the upper right), is combined with an unflinching depiction of Christian agony, sacrifice and sorrow. This has been related to the death of his first wife, Brenda Mark, in 1960 and his own experiences of the Second World War.

Philipson returned to the work in 1980. He significantly changed the generally blue palette of the original, adding the yellow sections to either side of the rose window and darkening the ground behind Christ to shades of sombre greys and browns. Lady Philipson, the artist's widow, believes that on returning to the original painting he may have considered that it needed greater depth, as one of his over-riding artistic concerns was to create different spatial areas within the picture plane. As a result he reworked the panels and area behind the figure, creating a feeling of space and distance, so that the viewer can look through and beyond the image.[40]

Crucifixion is intended to be hung above normal eye level so that the viewer is forced to look up at the tortured figure of Christ, who is situated at the very forefront of the picture plane. This positioning also emphasises the suffering conveyed in His splayed fingers, stretched arms and tormented face, which is reduced to a gaping mouth and vicious crown of thorns.

Philipson had a successful and prestigious career. He exhibited regularly with The Scottish Gallery in Edinburgh and with Roland, Browse and Delbanco in London. He was elected to the major British arts institutions and served as president of the RSA between 1973 and 1983. He was knighted for service to the arts in Scotland in 1976. Retrospective exhibitions of his work were held in Dunfermline in 1970 and in Edinburgh in 1989 and 1999. He died in the capital in 1992.

JOHN QUINTON PRINGLE

Born Glasgow 1864; died Glasgow 1925
Studied Glasgow School of Art 1885–92

Portrait of May (Mary Boyd), 1923
Oil on canvas, 30.5 × 25.4
Purchased 1972 with 50% NFA grant
13–1972

Pringle was born in Glasgow and served an apprenticeship with a local optician. In 1885 he won a bursary which allowed him to take evening classes at Glasgow School of Art, which he continued until 1892.

In 1896 Pringle opened an optical and scientific repair shop in Glasgow which he ran until retirement in 1923. He painted in the early mornings and in the evenings. As a result his output was small, but without the necessity to earn a living from his art, Pringle was able to follow his own interests and was little concerned with promoting and selling his work.

For a number of years Pringle's sister Mary kept house for him and assisted in the shop. Her death in 1911 came as a great shock and thereafter Pringle's lifestyle became increasingly austere. From 1911 until 1920, struggling to keep up with the demands of the business, Pringle painted almost exclusively in watercolour. However, a trip to Whalsay, Shetland, in 1921 inspired his return to the use of oils and the following year the only solo exhibition of his work held during his lifetime was mounted at Glasgow School of Art. It received public and critical acclaim and this, combined with ill-health, led to his retirement in 1923.

Some six months later he painted *Portrait of May (Mary Boyd)*. This painting is a gem-like example of Pringle's later, freer pointillist style, in which blocks of colour are fastidiously applied onto the small scale canvas. He is not likely to have seen much work by the neo-impressionists who are credited with inventing the technique, except perhaps a handful of examples by Henri Eugène Augustin Le Sidaner (1862–1939) shown at the Glasgow Institute. As a result it could be argued that he arrived at this approach, considered extreme at the time, by applying the skills required for the painstaking and detailed repair work in the shop to his painting. The fine, textured paint surface is enlivened by the delicate palette, based on tones of aqua-blue and green, but dominated by the rust-red of the sitter's hair.

Pringle wrote about the painting to the sitter's father:

I have not lost sight of the little head of May. I have spent a great deal of time with much care on the hair to try and be at one with it ... There is much I admire in May's head and sometimes I am very happy while I look at it. I have it in a black Dutch frame and for colour I am charmed with it.[41]

Pringle died in 1925, a lone figure whose important contribution to Scottish art is still in the process of being recognised. A centenary exhibition of his work was held at Kelvingrove Art Gallery and Museum, Glasgow, in 1964, a solo exhibition was held at the City Art Centre, Edinburgh, in 1973 and in 1981–2 a Scottish Arts Council exhibition of his work toured Britain.

ANNE REDPATH

Born Galashiels 1895; died Edinburgh 1965

Studied Edinburgh College of Art 1913–19 and Moray House College of Education, Edinburgh 1913–17

RSA ARA RBA ROI RWA

Eileen in a White Chair, 1953
[ILLUSTRATED]
Oil on board, 92.7 × 73.7
Purchased 1953 with the Morris Trust Fund
6–1953

Terraced Fields, Gran Canaria, 1960
Oil on canvas, 64 × 76.5
Bequest 2004 of David Murray Burns in memory of his father A.M. Burns of Dundee
2004–131

Plus four works on paper

Redpath was born in Galashiels. She studied simultaneously at Moray House College of Education, qualifying as a primary school teacher in 1917, and at Edinburgh College of Art, graduating in 1919. Two travelling scholarships allowed her to work in London, the Netherlands, France and Italy. In 1920 she married the architect James Beattie Michie (1891–1960) and they moved to northern France. Redpath continued to paint but devoted herself to her husband and their three sons. The family moved to the south of France in 1928 and remained in the country until 1934, when Redpath returned to Scotland with the children and Michie found a job in London.

Redpath soon fulfilled her early promise and quickly re-established her name in Scotland. In 1946 she exhibited in London for the first time and the following year had her first solo exhibition in Scotland. In 1949 she moved to Edinburgh where she lived for the rest of her life, becoming a cornerstone of the capital's cultural establishment. Thus began an extremely successful career, as Redpath maintained a healthy level of productivity, exhibited often and throughout Britain, and her work became eagerly sought after.

Redpath painted *Eileen in a White Chair* in 1953. The sitter is Eileen Michie (née Michie, 1927–2003, a distant relative) who married Redpath's third son, the artist David (b.1928) in 1951. David Michie has explained:

By profession a scientist, [Eileen] studied Biochemistry at the University of St Andrews. For many years she ran the clinical laboratory in the Simpson Memorial Maternity Pavilion of Edinburgh's Royal Infirmary ... The painting was carried out at my mother's house at 7 London Street in Edinburgh. There is no particular story about the environment shown, simply the furniture and rugs in my mother's sitting-room. The clothes Eileen was wearing my mother would have been familiar with and enjoyed the patterns they made ... The painting was made with Eileen posing from time to time and also without Eileen in front of her. Perhaps over a month, but not every day. No preliminary sketches or drawings were made. My mother did not regard herself as a portrait painter ... However she made quite a lot of portraits – which she regarded as paintings first and portraits second. [42]

In *Eileen in a White Chair* the smoothly painted pattern and muted grey and white tones of the sitter's outfit harmonise with the scumbled multi-coloured consistency of the rug and wall about her, whilst the chair in which she sits and the flowers on the nearby table add spatial depth to the concentration on surface texture elsewhere. The atmosphere is one of beauty and domestic calmness, recalling the work of the French artists Pierre Bonnard (1867–1947) and Edouard Vuillard (1868–1940).

Redpath's distinguished later career was characterised by a pattern of foreign travel and painting for regular exhibitions, even coronary thromboses in 1955 and 1959 failing to deter her. Following her death in 1965 a memorial exhibition was held at the RSA in 1965 to 1966, of which a selection then toured throughout Scotland. The Scottish National Gallery of Modern Art, Edinburgh, mounted a retrospective exhibition in 1997.

WILLIAM SCOTT

Born Greenock 1913; died Coleford, Somerset 1989

Studied Belfast College of Art 1928–31 and Royal
Academy Schools, London 1931–5

Taught Bath Academy of Art 1941–2 and 1946–56
and Royal Academy Schools, London 1962–81

RA

Angle, 1963
Oil on canvas, 86.4 × 111.8
Bequeathed 1969 by A.F.C. Turner and presented 1972
through the Contemporary Art Society
12–1972

Plus two works on paper

Scott was born in Greenock in 1913 and moved to Enniskillen, Northern Ireland, in 1924. He studied in Belfast and London and in 1938 moved to Pont-Aven in Brittany with his artist wife Mary Lucas (1912–1999). Shortly before the outbreak of war they returned to Britain. In 1942 Scott was drafted into the Royal Engineers, becoming friends with Talbert McLean when they were transferred to the ordnance section, stationed at Ruabon, north Wales. After the war Scott was appointed senior painting master at Bath Academy of Art, where he had taught from 1941 until 1942 and where he remained until 1956. During this decade the importance of colour in his work diminished as that of simplified form and surface texture increased and he emerged at the forefront of British abstraction.

By the early 1960s Scott had achieved an assured national and international standing. He had regular solo exhibitions at the Hanover Gallery in London and the Martha Jackson Gallery in New York. He participated in significant group shows in Europe, America and elsewhere and his work was featured in survey publications of contemporary art. With Kenneth Armitage (1916–2002) and Stanley William Hayter (1901–1988), Scott was chosen to represent Britain at the XXIX Venice Biennale and retrospectives of his work were held at the Kestner-Gesellschaft, Hannover, in 1960 and at the Kunsthalle, Berne and Ulster Museum, Belfast, in 1963.

Scott created *Angle* in 1963 and it was included in his solo exhibition at the Hanover Gallery that year. Most of the titles of the paintings shown referred to conceptual qualities or events, reflecting how Scott's work was changing at this time,

using a limited repertoire of non-representational forms to embrace abstraction to a greater extent than ever before, with a more painterly and less graphic approach. In *Angle*, semi-circles, triangles with rounded corners and a diabolo shape are loosely outlined with a free hand and filled in with generous, unpremeditated, uneven brushstrokes of paint. The forms appear to float over a neutral, flat background, often going right up to the canvas edge, suggesting movement, rhythm and their existence beyond the picture frame. There is no central, focal point in the image which instead consists of the subtle contrast between the cream and white tones and the dominance of the black elements in an asymmetrical composition. The meditative, abstract quality of the painting reveals Scott's kinship with his artist friends Patrick Heron (1920–1999), Terry Frost (1915–2003) and Mark Rothko (1903–1970).

Shortly after painting *Angle*, Scott took up a twelve-month residency in West Berlin, run by the German Academic Exchange Service (DAAD), during which his work continued to develop dramatically. He returned to Britain in 1965 where his career proceeded apace. In 1966 he was created CBE and in 1972 and 1986 retrospective exhibitions were mounted at the Tate Gallery, London, and the Ulster Museum, Belfast, respectively. In 1984 Scott was elected to the Royal Academy, having been a visiting tutor at the Academy Schools from 1962 until 1981. He won prizes at the Academy's Summer Exhibitions of 1984 and 1985. Following his death in 1989 a memorial exhibition was held as part of the 1990 Summer Exhibition.

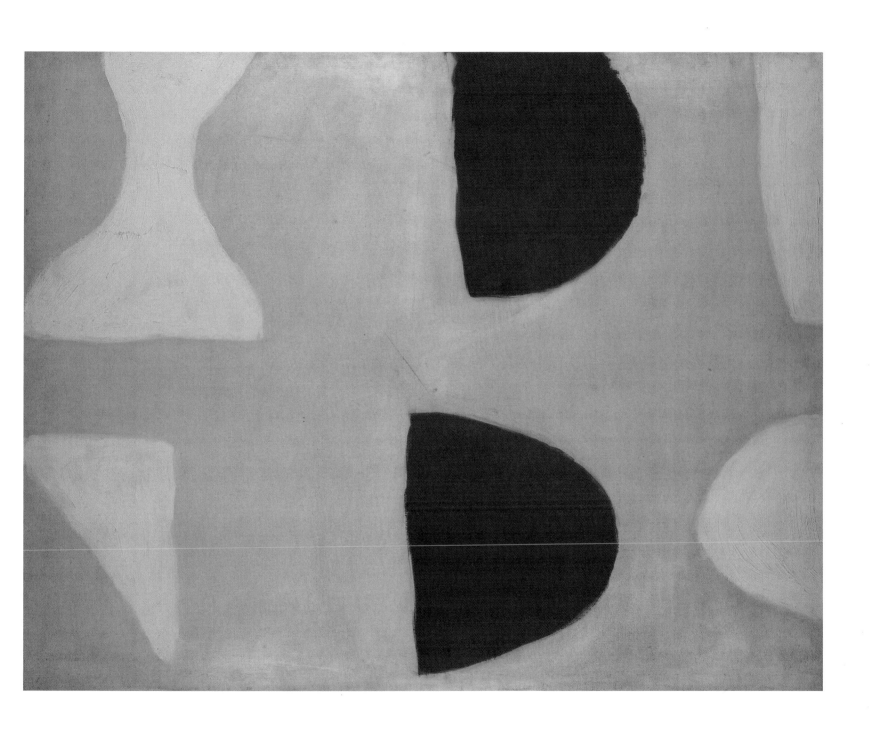

NOTES

Unless otherwise stated, letters and e-mails referred to are to Alice Strang and are in the accession files of McManus Galleries and Museum, Dundee.

1. Letter of 28 January 2006

2. Patrick Elliott, *Edward Baird 1904–1949*, Scottish National Gallery of Modern Art, Edinburgh, 1992, p.11

3. E-mail of 26 January 2006

4. Ibid.

5. Interview with Alice Strang of 12 January 2006

6. Letter of 5 January 2006 and interview with Alice Strang of 1 February 2006

7. Dave Taylor, 'Picture of the Month June 2000: Bill Burns (1921–1972) *Seatown VI*', Aberdeen Art Gallery Display Text

8. Letter of 'Sunday 18 August'

9. See file GMA A37/1/470, Richard Demarco Archive, Scottish National Gallery of Modern Art, Edinburgh

10. Letter of 12 January 2006

11. Letter of 11 January 2006

12. Quoted by Cordelia Oliver, 'Introduction', *Crawford and Company Selected Work 1928–1978*, Third Eye Centre, Glasgow, 1978, p.8

13. Interview with Alice Strang of 17 February 2006

14. See letter from David Walker, Scottish Development Department, to William Hardie, Dundee Art Gallery, of 5 May 1975

15. See William Hardie, 'A note on the Futurist paintings of Stanley Cursiter', *Stanley Cursiter Centenary Exhibition*, Piers Arts Centre, Stromness, 1987, p.12

16. Extracts from the artist's journal by permission of Amanda Brown

17. Extract from John Duncan papers, National Libraries of Scotland (Acc.6866)

18. Benno Schotz, 'Introduction', *Alan Fletcher 1930–1958 A Memorial Exhibition*, The Arts Council Scottish Committee, McLellan Galleries, Glasgow, June 1959, non-paginated

19. Letter to the director, Museums and Art Galleries Department, The Corporation of Dundee of 18 June 1971

20. Chloë Gunn, 'A Memoir', *Sir James Gunn 1893–1964*, Scottish National Portrait Gallery, Edinburgh, 1994, p.34

21. Letter of 4 January 2006

22. Letter to Anna Robertson, McManus Galleries and Museum, of 29 January 1999

23. As stated in *Private View*, a 1960 John Schlessinger film for the BBC *Monitor* series

24. Letter of 8 December 2005

25. Letter to William Hardie, Keeper of Art, Dundee Art Gallery, of 2 August 1972

26. Letter of 10 January 2006

27. Quoted by Cordelia Oliver, *Jack Knox: Paintings and Drawings 1960–83*, Scottish Arts Council touring exhibition, 1983–4, p.24

28. Letter of 4 February 2006

29. Patrick Elliott, *William McCance 1894-1970*, Edinburgh, 1990, p.7

30. Letter of 27 December 2005

31. Ibid.

32. Letter of 4 January 2006

33. Duncan Macmillan, *The Art of Will Maclean: Symbols of Survival*, Edinburgh, 2002, p.32

34. E-mail of 9 January 2006

35. In conversation with Clara Young, McManus Galleries and Museum; see Victoria Keller and Clara Young, *Alberto Morrocco*, Edinburgh, 1993, p.58

36. Ibid., p.47

37. Quoted in James McIntosh Patrick interview series, *Dundee Courier*, summer of 1967

38. Ibid.

39. Quoted in Stanley Cursiter, *Peploe: An intimate memoir of an artist and of his work*, Edinburgh, 1947, p.73

40. Interview with Alice Strang of 7 February 2006

41. Letter to James Boyd, Dennistoun, of 9 September 1923

42. Letter of 8 January 2006

James Howie, *Island*, 1969 [detail]

COPYRIGHT CREDITS